THE NEW HR LEADER'S 90 DAY PLAYBOOK:

Practical Strategies to Grow Your Leadership and Impact Organizational Success

By Dr. Sheila Gilbert

ISBN: 979-8-9997791-1-3

Printed in the United States of America

Visit www.Drsheilagilbert.com For free resources to help you access and begin your leadership journey.

Cover Design: Parks Media

Editor: Dr. Joel Boyce of JCB Educational Services

DEDICATION

To the next generation of HR professionals—

May you lead with courage, advocate with compassion, and shape workplaces where people and purpose thrive. This work is dedicated to your continued growth and impact in the field.

CONTENTS

INTRODUCTION:
NAVIGATING THE TURBULENCE OF HR LEADERSHIP

"Fasten your seatbelts. Turbulence doesn't mean we're crashing—it means we're climbing."

The captain's voice crackles over the intercom as the plane shudders. Outside the window, dark clouds press against the aircraft. The "Fasten Seatbelt" sign illuminates with a soft ding that belies the anxiety it triggers. Your knuckles whiten as you grip the armrests. The passenger beside you closes her eyes, while across the aisle, a seasoned business traveler continues typing on his laptop, seemingly oblivious to the violent rocking.

This scene—the turbulence at 35,000 feet—is perhaps the perfect metaphor for your first 90 days as a human resources leader.

You've accepted your new HR leadership role. Congratulations! Now the real work begins. While your organization may have an onboarding process in place, the sobering truth is that most companies provide inadequate transition support for leaders, particularly in HR. Many HR leaders report receiving little to no structured onboarding when assuming their roles. The result? Extended time to productivity, missed early opportunities, and in some cases, derailed careers.

This chapter introduces a powerful solution—the self-directed HR leadership onboarding plan. Unlike standard onboarding checklists, a self-leadership onboarding plan is a strategic roadmap that you develop and control. It's a comprehensive framework that addresses not only what you need to learn but also how you'll establish credibility, build critical relationships, deliver early wins, and lay the foundation for long-term success. Most importantly, it puts you in control of your leadership journey rather than leaving your transition to chance or others' limited expectations.

By creating your own structured 30-60-90 day plan, you accomplish something powerful—you establish yourself as a strategic, proactive leader before implementing a single HR initiative. The very act of presenting a thoughtful onboarding plan signals to your organization that you approach leadership with intention and foresight—qualities essential for exceptional HR leadership.

I've had many "first" journeys in my life—stepping onto a college campus for the first time, nervously navigating the complexities of graduate school, and walking the halls of law school with both ambition and trepidation. The first day of marriage and motherhood brought their own lessons, each requiring a shift in perspective and a recalibration of priorities. Each of these milestones pushed me beyond my comfort zone and forced me to confront self-doubt, fear, and uncertainty. The first ninety days as an HR professional requires that same push.

Throughout this book, we'll return to this flying metaphor because it captures the essence of HR leadership in transition. Like aviation, HR leadership combines technical skill with environmental awareness. It requires both confidence and humility. It demands preparation while acknowledging that no amount of planning can eliminate all turbulence. Most importantly, it reminds us that the bumps along the way are not evidence of failure but simply part of climbing to cruising altitude.

The chapters that follow provide your flight plan for the first 90 days as an HR leader. We begin with the elevated mindset essential for navigating complex organizational terrains. We examine the crash reports of those who didn't complete their journeys successfully, not to instill fear but to highlight the navigation errors that led to their difficulty. We then provide detailed guidance for creating your personal onboarding flight plan, accelerating your learning curve, and making a powerful first impression when you take the controls.

From there, we explore the instrumentation of emotional intelligence and relationship management that will guide you through low-visibility conditions. We establish protocols for setting expectations, solving problems collaboratively, and maintaining momentum even when organizational headwinds intensify. Throughout this book, we focus on practical strategies that acknowledge the realities of HR leadership while empowering you to rise above the turbulence.

In my journey as an HR professional, I've learned that while preparation and planning are important, the most crucial element of any journey is mindset. The way you think determines how you respond to challenges, how you process setbacks, and how you create opportunities. Success isn't about avoiding failure—it's about having the mental strength to get up after you fall, adjust your course, and continue your ascent.

The strategies outlined in this book are the same ones I used to shift my perspective, build confidence, and ultimately thrive in my HR leadership role. Once I embraced this new mindset, I saw measurable growth, both professionally and personally. I was able to deliver results with the same intensity, innovation, and impact as I had in my previous roles. More importantly, this journey led me to the fulfillment of my true purpose—educating, empowering, and equipping the next generation of HR leaders.

Life does not come with a play-by-play guide or guarantees, but in this age of technology and openness of information, we can ensure that we are adequately prepared for each journey by utilizing strategic tools to help us along the way. This book is designed to give you actionable strategies to elevate your mindset and set you on a course for sustainable success. It will challenge you to shift your perspective, embrace growth, and lead with confidence.

I wrote this book because I believe in the transformative power of skilled HR leadership. Organizations desperately need HR leaders who can navigate complexity, build authentic relationships, and align people strategies with business objectives. They need professionals who understand that HR isn't just about managing human resources—it's about cultivating human potential. The world needs your leadership flight to succeed, perhaps now more than ever.

Fasten your seatbelt. Embrace the turbulence as evidence that you're climbing, not crashing. Trust the flight plan we'll develop together, and remember that on the other side of these clouds lies the clear blue sky of impactful HR leadership. Your destination is worth the journey, and this book is your navigation system for getting there.

Now, take a deep breath. Embrace this moment. You are standing at the beginning of a transformative journey. You have the power to elevate your mindset, redefine your leadership approach, and make a lasting impact. Log onto my website for a free leadership assessment tool to help determine your leadership strengths and areas for growth- www.Drsheilagilbert.com. Welcome aboard.

CHAPTER 1:
UNDERSTANDING WHY HR LEADERS FAIL

THE ALTITUDE OF LEADERSHIP

> *"Your first 90 days as an HR leader aren't just a probation period—they're your runway to sustainable success or spectacular failure."*

Leadership transitions are precarious journeys. When new leaders struggle to find their footing, the impact ripples throughout their teams and across the organization. We all know the adage: people don't leave bad companies; they leave bad managers.However, what many don't realize is how quickly this downward spiral can begin and how preventable it often is.

The turbulence of leadership transition claims countless careers each year, with nearly 40% of new leaders failing within their first 18 months. For HR leaders specifically, this failure rate is particularly troubling, as they are expected to be the stewards of organizational culture, talent development, and leadership excellence. When they fail, the ripple effects extend far beyond their individual careers.

MY PERSONAL DESCENT INTO THE DANGER ZONE

I remember the day clearly. After working in HR for several years, handling everything from benefits administration to case management, I walked into my office to find my job description had been completely revamped. Overnight, I was tasked with overseeing a new function in an area where I had zero experience—a highly regulated function with compliance implications that could impact the entire organization.

There was no formal training provided. My supervisor, while well-intentioned, was a micromanager who had very little insight or knowledge of the area herself. The processes and procedures I inherited were dysfunctional at best, nonexistent at worst. There was no transition plan, no subject matter expert to consult and mounting pressure to deliver results immediately.

It was, by any objective measure, a recipe for failure. The turbulence indicators were flashing red across every dashboard, yet failing was simply not an option—not for the organization that needed this function to work, not for the team members looking to me for leadership, and certainly not for my own career trajectory.

This scenario—being thrust into leadership without adequate preparation or support—is one that countless HR professionals face. What separates those who crash and burn from those who successfully navigate the turbulence? That's precisely what this chapter will explore.

THE FOUR FAILURE PATTERNS OF NEW HR LEADERS

Before we can develop strategies to succeed, we must understand precisely why so many HR leaders fail during their critical first 90 days. Through my research and experience in coaching hundreds of HR professionals through transitions, I've identified four primary failure patterns that consistently emerge.

1. Identity Crisis: Failing to Make the Mental Shift from Doer to Leader

Many new HR leaders are promoted based on their technical excellence—their ability to manage complex benefits programs, navigate delicate employee relations issues, or design effective talent acquisition strategies. Others find themselves in leadership positions due to strong internal relationships or networking abilities rather than a demonstrated leadership capability. Regardless of how you arrived in your role, leadership requires a fundamentally different mindset. Transition failures often happen because new leaders misunderstand the essential demands of the situation or lack the skill and flexibility to adapt to them.

For HR leaders specifically, this means recognizing that your value is no longer primarily in your technical expertise or relationships but in your ability to build a high-performing team, align HR strategy with business objectives, and influence the executive team. When HR leaders cling to their technical contributor identity or rely too heavily on personal connections rather than leadership competencies, they create bottlenecks, micromanage their teams, and fail to establish strategic credibility with senior leadership. Those promoted through relationships often struggle even more with this transition, as they may have bypassed opportunities to develop critical leadership skills along the way.

2. Cultural Misalignment: Failing to Read and Adapt to Organizational Context

The second failure pattern emerges from what my research shows is the single most common reason HR leaders derail: cultural incompatibility. Leadership roles require more than just the right skill set; they necessitate a matching working style, decision-making approach, and collaboration capacity that aligns with the organization's culture.

HR leaders face a unique challenge here because they are often expected to be both guardians of the existing culture and agents of cultural change. When they misread the unwritten rules, power dynamics, and cultural expectations—or when they attempt to drive change too quickly without building the necessary coalitions—they isolate themselves and lose organizational trust.

3. Credibility Collapse: Failing to Establish Trust and Influence

The third failure pattern revolves around the critical currency of HR leadership: credibility. HR leaders must quickly establish trust across multiple stakeholder groups—the executive team, peer leaders, their direct reports, and the broader employee population.

When new HR leaders make early missteps in communication, fail to demonstrate business acumen, or cannot translate HR initiatives into business impact, they experience what I call a "credibility collapse." Once this occurs, even technically sound HR programs will face resistance, and the leader's ability to influence organizational decisions diminishes rapidly.

4. Execution Entropy: Failing to Drive Visible Results

The final failure pattern occurs when HR leaders cannot translate their vision and strategies into tangible outcomes within the crucial first 90 days. While HR initiatives often require time to show full impact, new leaders must demonstrate early wins that build momentum and confidence.

When HR leaders get trapped in analysis paralysis, fail to prioritize effectively, or become distracted by organizational politics, they fall victim to "execution entropy"—a gradual decay of focus and impact that undermines their leadership position before it's fully established. Visit <u>www.Drsheilagilbert.com</u> to identify your ideal leadership style and approach to help eliminate these barriers.

THE HR LEADER'S FLIGHT PLAN: SEVEN STRATEGIES TO SOAR IN YOUR FIRST 90 DAYS

Now that we've identified the primary reasons HR leaders fail, let's explore seven specific strategies to navigate these challenges successfully. Each strategy is designed to address one or more of the failure patterns we've discussed.

Strategy 1: Recalibrate Your Leadership Identity

The shift from technical HR expert to HR leader requires a fundamental recalibration of your professional identity. This isn't about abandoning your expertise—it's about expanding your self-concept to embrace your new role as a strategic leader.

Action Steps:

- Conduct a leadership identity audit. List the activities that occupied most of your time in your previous role, then consciously identify which of these you need to delegate or deprioritize.

- Schedule weekly "strategic thinking time" during which you focus exclusively on leadership questions rather than technical HR issues.

- Identify an executive mentor outside of HR who can help you develop a broader leadership perspective.

- Practice the phrase, "What do you think we should do?" when team members bring you problems rather than immediately offering solutions.

Remember, your success is no longer measured primarily by your individual contributions but by the collective performance of your team and the strategic impact of HR on the organization.

Strategy 2: Develop Cultural Intelligence and Adaptability

Understanding the written and unwritten rules of your organization is critical to your success as an HR leader. You need to become a cultural anthropologist, studying the norms, values, and power dynamics that shape how work actually gets done.

Action Steps:

- Create a cultural map of your organization, identifying key influencers (who may not be the same as formal leaders), decision-making styles, and communication preferences.

- Schedule "listening tours" with long-tenured employees across different departments to understand the organization's history and unwritten rules.

- Identify the "cultural carriers"—those individuals who exemplify the organization's values—and observe how they navigate challenging situations.

- Before implementing any significant HR changes, test your approach with a trusted cultural advisor who can help you anticipate resistance and refine your messaging.

Cultural intelligence isn't about conforming to every aspect of the existing culture—it's about understanding it deeply enough to know how to effectively introduce change without triggering unnecessary resistance.

Strategy 3: Build a Credibility Bank Through Business Acumen

HR leaders often struggle to establish credibility because they speak the language of HR rather than the language of business. Building a "credibility bank" requires demonstrating that you understand the organization's business model, competitive challenges, and financial realities.

Action Steps:

- Immerse yourself in the organization's business model. Understand how the company makes money, who its key customers are, and what drives profitability.

- Schedule meetings with finance leaders to understand the key metrics that matter most to the organization.

- When presenting HR initiatives, always frame them in terms of business impact—increased productivity, reduced turnover costs, enhanced customer satisfaction, or other business-relevant outcomes.

- Develop a "business impact dashboard" for your HR function that demonstrates how HR activities contribute to key business metrics.

Remember, in the first 90 days, your credibility will be assessed less on your HR expertise (which is assumed) and more on your ability to align HR strategies with business priorities.

Strategy 4: Master Strategic Stakeholder Management

HR leaders operate at the intersection of multiple stakeholder groups, each with their own expectations, priorities, and communication styles. Successful navigation requires intentional stakeholder management.

Action Steps:

- Create a comprehensive stakeholder map, identifying key individuals and groups who will influence your success. Include their priorities, pain points, and preferred communication styles.

- Establish regular touchpoints with critical stakeholders, particularly the executive team and influential line managers.

- Develop tailored "value propositions" for different stakeholder groups that explain how your HR leadership will address their specific challenges.

- Identify potential allies and resistors for key initiatives and develop strategies to leverage support and mitigate opposition.

The most successful HR leaders recognize that different stakeholders require different approaches, and they consciously adapt their communication and influence strategies accordingly.

Strategy 5: Implement the 30-30-30 Execution Framework

To avoid execution entropy, successful HR leaders divide their first 90 days into three distinct phases, each with specific objectives and deliverables.

Action Steps:

First 30 Days: Listen and Learn

- Conduct a comprehensive HR audit, evaluating current programs, policies, and team capabilities.

- Identify immediate pain points that can be addressed quickly to build credibility.

- Establish relationships with key stakeholders and gather diverse perspectives on HR priorities.

Second 30 Days: Align and Architect

- Develop a strategic HR plan aligned with business priorities.

- Identify 2-3 "quick wins" that demonstrate value and build momentum.

- Begin restructuring any dysfunctional HR processes that impede effectiveness.

Final 30 Days: Activate and Accelerate

- Implement your quick wins and communicate successes broadly.

- Finalize your longer-term HR strategy and socialize it with key stakeholders.

- Establish metrics and accountability systems for ongoing HR initiatives.

This phased approach ensures that you maintain focus and momentum throughout the critical first 90 days while building a foundation for longer-term success.

Strategy 6: Cultivate Your Team as Your Force Multiplier

Your HR team will ultimately determine your success or failure as a leader. Investing in their development and engagement from day one is not optional—it's essential.

Action Steps:

- Conduct individual meetings with each team member to understand their strengths, aspirations, and perspectives on HR challenges.

- Assess team capabilities objectively and develop targeted development plans that align individual growth with organizational needs.

- Create opportunities for team members to demonstrate their expertise and contribute to strategic initiatives.

- Address performance issues promptly and directly, recognizing that your credibility as a leader depends on having a high-performing team.

Remember that your team members are not just resources to execute your vision—they are your critical partners in navigating the organizational landscape and delivering HR excellence.

Strategy 7: Develop Resilience Through Self-Leadership

The turbulence of leadership transition can be emotionally and intellectually taxing. Sustainable success requires intentional self-leadership and resilience-building practices.

Action Steps:

- Establish clear boundaries between your work and personal life to ensure you have the energy and perspective needed for leadership challenges.

- Identify your personal "derailers"—the stress responses or behavioral patterns that emerge under pressure—and develop specific strategies to manage them.

- Create a personal board of directors—mentors and trusted advisors who can provide perspective and guidance during challenging situations.

- Institute regular reflection practices to evaluate your progress, adjust your approach, and maintain focus on key priorities.

Self-leadership isn't self-indulgent. It's a strategic necessity for maintaining the clarity, energy, and perspective required for HR leadership excellence.

FROM POTENTIAL FAILURE TO SPECTACULAR SUCCESS

When I faced my own leadership challenge—thrust into an unfamiliar, highly regulated area with minimal support—I drew on these exact strategies to navigate the turbulence. I recognized that my technical HR skills alone wouldn't save me. Instead, I needed to radically shift my approach.

I immersed myself in learning the regulatory requirements while simultaneously building a network of allies who could help me navigate the organization's culture. I was transparent about my knowledge gaps but confident in my ability to lead the team through the transition. Rather than pretending to have all the answers, I engaged the team in collaborative problem solving to redesign dysfunctional processes.

Within 90 days, we had established a clear compliance framework, rebuilt key processes, and demonstrated tangible improvements in operational metrics. What began as a potential career catastrophe became one of my most significant leadership achievements, not because I magically became a subject matter expert overnight, but because I applied the leadership strategies that separate successful transitions from failed ones.

YOUR FLIGHT PLAN FOR SUCCESS

The turbulence of HR leadership transitions is real and substantial. The statistics on leadership failure are sobering, and the examples of derailed careers are plentiful, but failure is not inevitable. By understanding the common pitfalls and intentionally implementing the strategies we've explored, you can navigate the challenges successfully and emerge as a transformative HR leader.

As you prepare for your own leadership journey, remember that the factors that will determine your success or failure have less to do with your technical HR expertise and more to do with how you navigate the leadership transition itself. Many talented HR professionals have stumbled during their first 90 days, but by applying these strategies, you can chart a different course.

The next chapter awaits. Fasten your seatbelt, embrace the challenge, and prepare for takeoff. Your leadership journey begins now.

CHAPTER 2:
THE ELEVATED MINDSET OF SUCCESSFUL HR LEADERS

———

THE ALTITUDE OF LEADERSHIP

"Your mind is the control tower of your leadership flight path—program it for altitude, not turbulence."

Picture yourself on day one as an HR leader. In front of you is a mountain of challenges—perhaps an employee engagement score at an all-time low, a compensation structure that hasn't been updated in years, and a leadership team that views HR as little more than an administrative function. The turbulence ahead is undeniable, yet how you perceive these challenges will determine whether you experience them as overwhelming obstacles or energizing opportunities. The strategies listed in chapter one will only be effective if executed with the proper mindset.

Leadership doesn't begin with action—it begins with perception. How you interpret your circumstances determines your response to them. Before you implement a single policy or facilitate a single meeting, your mindset has already set your leadership trajectory. It's not the situations we face as HR leaders that define us; it's the lens through which we view them and the altitude at which we choose to fly.

"Mind over matter" is more than just a motivational phrase—it's a leadership philosophy that governs success in the HR function. Your thoughts shape your reality. Your reality influences your actions. Your actions define your legacy. Leadership begins in the mind—what you believe about yourself, your abilities, and your capacity to navigate challenges will determine your success and that of those you lead.

THE SEEDS OF AN ELEVATED MINDSET

The journey to an elevated mindset often begins in the most unexpected places. For me, it started in the small town of Canton, Mississippi where the humid air carried both the weight of history and the whispers of possibility.

Raised by my grandparents during the academic year, I learned early that education wasn't just about books and grades—it was the key to unlocking doors that seemed forever sealed. My grandmother, despite her eighth-grade education, instilled in me a deep reverence for learning. My grandfather, armed with only a middle school education, reinforced those lessons through unwavering work ethic and determination.

Summers spent with my great-grandmother and great-great-grandmother in Louisiana further shaped my perspective. Though they had little formal education, their wisdom was profound. Their home was a sanctuary where love, hard work, and resilience weren't just words—they were the foundation of daily life.

One summer, my great-grandmother spoke words that would become the cornerstone of my leadership philosophy. She said, "You are destined for greatness, and you are equipped to overcome any and all obstacles." Simple, yet powerful, these words reshaped my understanding of possibility. Years later, as I faced professional challenges, they became my guiding light through storms of doubt and uncertainty.

YOUR PERCEPTIONS CREATE YOUR HR REALITY

The most powerful lesson I've learned in my HR leadership journey is this: how you perceive challenges fundamentally alters your ability to address them. When you view organizational problems as indictments of your leadership, you become defensive and reactive. When you view them as opportunities to create value, you become strategic and proactive.

This principle became painfully clear when I was suddenly reassigned to one of the least visible areas in HR. The functions were merely repetitive administrative duties with no real decision-making authority. The scope of my responsibility was decimated. The fall from grace was great. Holding a doctorate degree in organizational culture, having led teams upward of 20 professionals previously, being seen as an authority in my field and a stellar leader, I was now reduced to little to no authority.

What could have been perceived as a career-ending setback became, through conscious reframing, an opportunity to shine. Rather than viewing this reassignment as punishment or failure, I chose to see it as a challenge to transform the overlooked function into a showcase of excellence. I approached administrative work with the same strategic mindset I had applied to larger initiatives, finding opportunities for innovation and impact where others saw only mundane tasks.

Within eighteen months, I had reimagined the function, created measurable value, and drawn positive attention from my new supervisor. The reassignment that was intended to diminish my influence instead became a platform for demonstrating my adaptability and commitment to organizational excellence—all because I consciously chose an elevated perception of the situation.

THE FOUR PILLARS OF AN ELEVATED HR LEADERSHIP MINDSET

An elevated mindset isn't something you're born with. It's something you consciously develop. Through working with other HR leaders, I've identified four foundational pillars that support elevated thinking:

Pillar 1: Possibility-Focused Orientation

HR leaders with elevated mindsets train themselves to see possibilities where others see problems. They ask "What could be?" before "What's wrong?" This isn't naive optimism. It's strategic reframing that expands solution space.

Pillar 2: Growth-Oriented Perspective

Traditional HR thinking often falls into the "fixed mindset" trap, viewing talent, capabilities, and organizational culture as relatively static. Leaders with elevated mindsets reject this limitation. They recognize that people, teams, and organizations are constantly evolving, and they leverage this natural momentum.

Pillar 3: Strategic Generosity

Elevated HR leadership requires moving beyond transactional thinking to strategic generosity, investing in others' success without immediate expectation of return. This mindset positions HR not as a service provider but as a value multiplier within the organization.

Pillar 4: Solutions Sovereignty

Many HR leaders unknowingly adopt a victim mindset when facing constraints, blaming limited budgets, resistant executives, or organizational politics for their inability to drive change. Leaders with elevated mindsets practice what I call "solutions sovereignty," taking complete ownership of finding solutions regardless of constraints.

MINDSET AS COMPETITIVE ADVANTAGE

Several years ago, I consulted with two HR leaders in competing organizations within the same industry. Both faced nearly identical challenges: tight labor markets, increasing compensation pressures, and leadership teams focused primarily on financial metrics.

The first leader constantly emphasized these constraints in team meetings, executive conversations, and planning sessions. Her default language pattern was, "We would implement this initiative, but..." Her team became known for explaining why strategic people initiatives couldn't succeed in their current environment.

The second leader acknowledged the same constraints but consistently reframed them. Her default language pattern was, "Given these market conditions, we have a unique opportunity to..." Instead of presenting problems to the executive team, she presented creative solutions that worked within constraints while moving the organization forward.

Within a year, the second organization had decreased turnover by 23% while the first continued to struggle.

The difference wasn't resources, market position, or HR team capabilities. The difference was mindset. The second leader had trained herself to perceive challenges as the context for innovation rather than reasons for limitation.

The journey to an elevated leadership mindset isn't accidental—it's intentional. Like physical fitness, mental elevation requires consistent, deliberate practice. The leaders who rise above the daily pressures of HR management to achieve true strategic impact are those who invest in their mental frameworks with the same discipline they bring to technical skill development.

THE ALTITUDE DECISION

As you navigate your first 90 days as an HR leader, remember that your most important leadership decision is the altitude at which you choose to fly. Will you navigate at ground level, dodging obstacles and focusing on immediate challenges, or will you elevate your perspective, seeing patterns, possibilities, and strategic opportunities invisible from lower altitudes?

Your team will rarely rise higher than your expectations. Your HR function will rarely deliver more value than your vision allows. Your influence will rarely exceed what your mindset makes possible. The decision to elevate your thinking isn't a one-time choice. It's a daily recommitment to seeing beyond the immediate, thinking beyond the conventional, and leading beyond the obvious.

The challenges of HR leadership in today's environment are real and substantial. Talent markets are competitive. Business demands are intense, and resources are often constrained, yet within these very challenges lies the opportunity for truly extraordinary HR leadership.

Your mind is the control tower of your leadership journey. Program it for altitude, not turbulence. Choose to see possibilities where others see problems. Commit to growth where others accept limitations. Practice generosity where others protect territory. Claim sovereignty over solutions where others point to constraints.

The elevated mindset isn't just a nice-to-have leadership quality. It's the fundamental differentiator between HR leaders who merely manage transactions and those who transform organizations. The altitude of your thinking determines the altitude of your leadership impact.

As this chapter closes, ask yourself, *What is one limiting belief I can release today? What is one challenge I can reframe as an opportunity? What is one daily practice I can adopt to elevate my leadership mindset?*

Your answers to these questions will set your leadership trajectory far more powerfully than any technical HR knowledge or skill. Choose elevation. Choose possibility. Choose the mindset that will define not just your first 90 days but your entire leadership legacy.

CHAPTER 3:
CREATING YOUR HR LEADERSHIP ONBOARDING PLAN

CHARTING YOUR LEADERSHIP COURSE

> *"The greatest irony in HR leadership is that we design onboarding plans for everyone except ourselves."*

You've accepted your new HR leadership role. Congratulations! Now, the real work begins. While your organization may have an onboarding process in place, the sobering truth is that most companies provide inadequate transition support for leaders, particularly in HR. Many HR leaders report receiving little to no structured onboarding when assuming their roles. The result? Less productivity, missed early opportunities, and in some cases, derailed careers.

This chapter introduces a powerful solution—the self-directed HR leadership onboarding plan. Unlike standard onboarding checklists, a self-leadership onboarding plan is a strategic roadmap that you develop and control. It's a comprehensive framework that addresses not just what you need to learn but how you'll establish credibility, build critical relationships, deliver early wins, and lay the foundation for long-term success. Most importantly, it puts you in control of your leadership journey rather than leaving your transition to chance or others' limited expectations.

By creating your own structured 30-60-90 day plan, you accomplish something powerful. You establish yourself as a strategic, proactive leader before implementing a single HR initiative. The very act of presenting a thoughtful onboarding plan signals to your organization that you approach leadership with intention and foresight–qualities that are essential for exceptional HR leadership. Let's start with the self audit checklist at www.Drsheilagilbert.com.

MY STRATEGIC APPROACH TO RECOVERY

When I was reassigned to the administrative function within HR, I did not immediately recognize this as an opportunity to demonstrate the transformative power of strategic leadership. It took me a while, but it finally dawned on me that although the role appeared limited on paper–with primarily administrative duties and reduced decision-making authority– it was the perfect canvas to showcase my capabilities. I viewed this transition as a strategic opportunity to apply my leadership expertise in a new context, drawing on both my experience leading teams and my academic background in organizational culture.

I recognized that my response to that situation would define not just my immediate future but potentially my entire career trajectory. Rather than submitting to circumstance, I created a detailed 30-60-90 day plan that approached this reassignment as if it were a coveted new leadership position.

In my first 30 days, I conducted a comprehensive assessment of the function, examining processes, identifying inefficiencies, and uncovering hidden opportunities for strategic impact. I scheduled individual meetings with key stakeholders to understand their perceptions of the function and their unmet needs. While many were surprised by my proactive approach to what they considered a "back-office" role, these conversations revealed critical gaps in service delivery and revealed untapped opportunities for collaboration.

During days 31-60, I developed and began implementing process improvements that delivered immediate efficiency gains. I reframed routine administrative tasks as critical infrastructure that supported organizational effectiveness. I meticulously documented the function's actual impact on business operations, creating visibility for work that had previously been overlooked. Most importantly, I began shifting stakeholder perceptions through consistent, excellence-focused communication that connected our administrative work to strategic business outcomes.

By days 61-90, I had completely reimagined the function's potential. I presented my supervisor with a vision for transforming these administrative processes into strategic enablers, backed by data from my assessment and early improvements. Rather than simply performing my assigned tasks, I had rewritten the role's possibilities. The function that was intended as a career sideline became a showcase for my leadership capabilities precisely because I approached it with a strategic onboarding mindset.

THE ONBOARDING PARADOX: PREPARE AS THOUGH NO ONE ELSE WILL

The most important lesson from my experience and those of countless HR leaders I've coached is that regardless of your organization's formal onboarding process, your transition success depends primarily on your own strategic approach. This isn't about compensating for organizational deficiencies. It's about taking ownership of your leadership journey from day one.

HR professionals excel at creating onboarding experiences for others, yet we rarely apply the same structured thinking to our own transitions. This paradox creates both vulnerability and opportunity. While most HR leaders navigate transitions through instinct and reaction, those who develop deliberate onboarding plans gain an immediate advantage that compounds throughout their tenure.

Your self-directed onboarding plan serves multiple purposes simultaneously. It accelerates your learning and integration. It demonstrates your strategic mindset. It establishes your leadership brand, and perhaps most importantly, it provides a structured framework for navigating the inevitable turbulence of leadership transitions.

STRATEGIC PLANNING:
THE ARCHITECTURE OF EFFECTIVE ONBOARDING

The key takeaway from my experiences is that effective leadership onboarding requires deliberate architecture—a structured approach that balances learning, relationship-building, and value delivery. Your self-directed onboarding plan should serve as both a navigational chart and accountability framework for your critical first three months.

The most effective HR leadership onboarding plans address five critical dimensions:

1. **Knowledge Acquisition**: What you need to learn about the business, culture, HR function, and key challenges

2. **Relationship Development**: How you'll build essential connections with stakeholders at all levels

3. **Value Creation**: What early wins you'll deliver to establish your credibility

4. **Team Alignment**: How you'll assess and develop your HR team

5. **Strategic Positioning**: How you'll elevate HR's organizational influence

ONBOARDING IN ACTION: MY 30-60-90 DAY SUCCESS STORY

When I developed my 30-60-90 day onboarding plan for that seemingly diminished administrative role, I approached it with the same strategic mindset I would apply to any significant leadership position. Here's how I structured my approach:

First 30 Days: The Assessment Phase

I began by conducting a thorough assessment of the administrative function, documenting processes, identifying inefficiencies, and connecting these administrative activities to broader business impacts that had previously gone unrecognized. I scheduled meetings with stakeholders who depended on these administrative services, asking probing questions about their needs, pain points, and perspectives on how the function could better support their objectives.

The assessment revealed something surprising. What appeared to be routine administrative work actually touched critical business processes that directly impacted operational effectiveness. The function's invisibility wasn't due to inherent insignificance but to a failure to connect administrative activities to strategic outcomes. This insight became the foundation for my transformation approach.

Days 31-60: The Alignment Phase

During the second month, I began implementing process improvements that delivered immediate efficiency gains. I reorganized workflows, eliminated redundant steps, and introduced simple technology solutions to automate repetitive tasks. These improvements freed time for more strategic activities while demonstrating my commitment to excellence.

Most importantly, I developed a new narrative for the function, explicitly connecting our administrative work to organizational effectiveness. Every communication, report, and interaction emphasized not just what we did but why it mattered to business outcomes. This narrative shift began transforming perceptions of both the function and my leadership.

Days 61-90: The Activation Phase

By the third month, I had developed a comprehensive vision for transforming the administrative function into a strategic enabler. I presented leadership with a proposal that reimagined the function's purpose, structure, and deliverables—all grounded in the business impact insights I had gathered during my assessment.

The proposal included metrics demonstrating the efficiency improvements already implemented and a roadmap for future transformation. What began as a perfunctory presentation of administrative activities became a compelling case for strategic evolution with me positioned as the natural leader for this transformation.

The results exceeded my most optimistic expectations. Within six months, what had been positioned as a career demotion became a showcase for my strategic leadership capabilities. The administrative function gained visibility as a critical business enabler, and my role expanded to include additional strategic responsibilities. Most importantly, I demonstrated that leadership impact depends not on formal authority but on strategic approach—a lesson that continues to guide my leadership philosophy. To access a free 30-60-90 Day Leadership Plan Template, log on to www. Drsheilagilbert.com.

YOUR ACTION PLAN: TAKING CONTROL

The journey to creating your own HR leadership onboarding plan begins now. Here are five immediate actions to take:

1. **Create Your Knowledge Acquisition Plan**: Identify what you need to learn about the business, culture, HR function, and strategic challenges. Create a structured approach to developing this knowledge during your first 90 days.

2. **Develop Your Stakeholder Map**: Identify the key individuals and groups whose support you'll need. Create a relationship development strategy for each stakeholder category.

3. **Identify Potential Quick Wins**: Based on available information, identify 3-5 opportunities to make an

early impact. Create a preliminary implementation plan for each opportunity.

4. **Assess Team Capabilities**: If you're inheriting a team, develop an approach for quickly assessing individual and collective capabilities. Create a preliminary team development strategy.

5. **Craft Your Strategic Narrative**: Develop the story you'll tell about HR's role and value. Create a communication plan for positioning HR as a strategic partner.

Remember, your onboarding plan is not just an operational tool. It's a strategic statement about your leadership approach. By developing a structured plan before your first day, you demonstrate the proactive, strategic mindset that distinguishes exceptional HR leaders.

The Self-Directed Journey to Leadership Excellence

As we conclude this chapter, remember this essential truth. In leadership transitions, the quality of your preparation determines the trajectory of your journey. Your self-directed onboarding plan is not just a tactical roadmap. It's a declaration of leadership intent and a foundation for sustainable success.

By taking control of your transition through deliberate planning, you shift from a passive participant to an active architect of your leadership journey. You demonstrate the strategic mindset that separates exceptional HR leaders from average ones, and you establish a foundation for influence that extends far beyond your formal authority.

The HR leaders who create the greatest organizational impact are not those with the most impressive credentials or the broadest technical expertise. They are those who approach leadership transitions with strategic intention. Your 30-60-90 day plan is your first and perhaps most important opportunity to demonstrate this strategic approach.

As you prepare to take the helm of your HR leadership role, commit to creating the onboarding experience you deserve. Develop your knowledge acquisition plan, map your stakeholder landscape, identify your quick wins, assess your team capabilities, and craft your strategic narrative. Then, navigate your transition with the confidence that comes from thorough preparation and clear direction.

Your leadership journey awaits. The path to extraordinary HR leadership begins now.

CHAPTER 4:
DAY ONE: ESTABLISHING CONFIDENCE AND AUTHORITY

THE POWER OF FIRST IMPRESSIONS

"You'll never get a second chance to establish your first presence. Day one isn't just another workday, It's the opening chapter of your leadership story."

The morning of your first day as an HR leader brings a unique convergence of opportunity and vulnerability. As you walk through those doors, eyes will follow you, conversations will pause momentarily, and minds will begin forming impressions that can either accelerate or impede your leadership journey. Research confirms what intuition suggests. First impressions form rapidly, persist tenaciously, and influence how all subsequent information about you is interpreted.

For HR leaders specifically, this first impression dynamic carries heightened significance. Unlike other functional leaders who may have the luxury of establishing their authority gradually through technical contributions, HR leaders are immediately thrust into the spotlight as cultural standard-bearers and people management exemplars. Your credibility as an HR leader who advises others on leadership effectiveness will be evaluated, in part, by how effectively you demonstrate leadership yourself, beginning with your very first interactions.

Many new HR leaders underestimate the strategic importance of day one, treating it as primarily administrative and procedural rather than as a critical leadership positioning opportunity. They focus on logistics and basic introductions while missing the chance to deliberately craft their leadership narrative and establish the foundation for their authority. This passive approach cedes control of a powerful leadership moment to chance and others' preconceptions.

This chapter provides a strategic framework for leveraging day one to establish the confidence and authority that will define your leadership tenure. We'll explore proven approaches for making powerful first impressions, setting the tone for your leadership and laying groundwork for sustained influence. You'll learn how to balance approachability with authority, demonstrate both competence and character, and begin establishing trust from your first interactions.

Your first day represents a unique moment when expectations are still forming, and possibilities remain wide open. By approaching it with strategic intent rather than passive participation, you create momentum that will carry forward throughout your critical first 90 days and beyond.

THE PREPARATION EDGE: CONFIDENCE BEGINS BEFORE DAY ONE

The foundation of day-one confidence isn't laid on day one. It's established in the days and weeks before you officially start. This principle became clear to me early in my HR leadership journey, and it has shaped my approach to every leadership transition since then.

Prior to beginning a particularly challenging faith-based HR leadership role, I recognized that I would be entering an environment where skepticism about HR's value was deeply entrenched. Previous HR leaders had been viewed as being disconnected from business realities, and expectations for meaningful contribution were low. I knew that overcoming this perception would require establishing credibility immediately.

Rather than waiting for formal onboarding, I initiated several strategic pre-boarding activities. I scheduled individual phone conversations with each executive team member, focusing not on HR-specific topics but on their business priorities and challenges. I reviewed key financial and strategic documents, preparing specific questions that demonstrated my business acumen. I researched industry trends and competitive dynamics, developing my perspective on how people strategies could address market challenges.

When I walked through the door on day one, I wasn't meeting key stakeholders for the first time. I was continuing conversations that had already begun. I wasn't learning about the business from square one. I was building on a foundation of knowledge that was already established. This preparation created a palpable difference in my confidence level, which in turn shaped how others perceived my authority from our very first interactions.

The principle here is straightforward but powerful—day-one confidence doesn't emerge spontaneously. It stems from deliberate preparation that enables you to engage substantively from your first moments in the role. The more thoroughly you prepare, the more naturally confidence flows, and the more authentically your leadership authority is established.

The First Day Authority Framework

Establishing authority on day one requires a deliberate approach that balances multiple dimensions of leadership presence. The First Day Authority Framework addresses five key elements:

1. **Physical Presence**: How you present yourself visually and the nonverbal signals you convey

2. **Communication Approach**: How you express ideas and engage with others

3. **Relational Positioning**: How you establish the nature of your relationships with different stakeholders

4. **Knowledge Demonstration**: How you selectively showcase relevant expertise

5. **Intention Setting**: How you signal your leadership priorities and approach

PHYSICAL PRESENCE:
THE VISUAL FOUNDATION OF AUTHORITY

Your physical presence—how you carry yourself, dress, and occupy space—creates immediate impressions about your confidence and authority. While substance ultimately matters more than style, ignoring the impact of physical presence handicaps your leadership effectiveness unnecessarily.

- Dress slightly more formally than the organization's norm for your first day. This demonstrates respect for the importance of the occasion without creating excessive distance. Research the organization's dress code in advance and aim for the upper end of appropriate rather than a dramatic departure from norms.

- Practice deliberate body language that conveys both confidence and openness.

- Take control of your physical environment where possible.

Action Step: Before your first day, conduct a presence audit. Plan your first-day attire thoughtfully, considering both organizational norms and the impression you want to create.

COMMUNICATION APPROACH: THE VERBAL DIMENSION OF AUTHORITY

How you communicate—your word choice, pacing, listening patterns, and questioning approaches—directly impacts perceptions of your authority and confidence. Effective leaders modulate their communication to balance competence demonstration with connection building.

- Prepare key messages in advance for predictable first-day scenarios.

- Establish yourself as a leader who truly listens.

Action Step: Practice speaking with clarity and confidence. Before engaging in key conversations, take a moment to reflect on the core message you want to convey. Use concise, purposeful language that aligns with your leadership objectives.

RELATIONAL POSITIONING: ESTABLISHING LEADERSHIP CONNECTIONS

The nature of the relationships you begin forming on day one significantly impacts your long-term authority. The most effective HR leaders strategically balance approachability with appropriate professional distance, establishing connections that enable influence without undermining their leadership positioning.

- Build influence by genuinely listening to others and valuing their input

- Engage others in decisions to create a sense of shared responsibility while maintaining authority

- Navigate relationships effectively by balancing empathy with firm leadership

Action Step: Assess the dynamics of each relationship and adjust your approach to balance approachability with authority. Practice active listening, engage others in decision-making where appropriate, and set clear boundaries to establish your leadership presence while fostering trust and respect.

KNOWLEDGE DEMONSTRATION: SELECTIVE EXPERTISE SHARING

How and when you demonstrate expertise on your first day significantly impacts others' perceptions of your competence and credibility. The goal is balanced knowledge sharing that establishes your capabilities without appearing arrogant or disconnected from organizational realities.

- Selectively offer perspectives that add immediate value.

- Balance expertise with an evident commitment to understanding.

Action Step: Ensure that your knowledge is shared in a way that adds immediate value while also showing a genuine willingness to learn and understand the organization's unique challenges.

INTENTION SETTING: SIGNALING YOUR LEADERSHIP APPROACH

The expectations and intentions you communicate on day one establish the foundation for how your leadership will be perceived and experienced. Effective HR leaders use this opportunity to deliberately set the tone for their tenure.

- Begin sharing your perspective on HR's potential contribution.

- Signal the values that will guide your leadership.

- Begin establishing mutual expectations.

Action Step: Clearly articulate your vision, highlighting how it will contribute to broader goals. Demonstrate your core values through your actions and words, ensuring they align with the organization's culture. Set clear expectations for collaboration, performance, and growth, creating a transparent and cohesive leadership environment from the outset.

AUTHORITY THROUGH AUTHENTIC LEADERSHIP

Throughout this chapter, we've explored strategies for establishing confidence and authority on day one. It's important to emphasize that true authority stems from authenticity rather than performance. The most effective HR leaders don't adopt artificial personas. They present their best authentic selves aligned with organizational needs.

I learned this lesson early in my career when I observed two new HR leaders take dramatically different approaches. The first attempted to establish authority through an authoritarian style misaligned with both her natural demeanor and the organization's culture. The second demonstrated quiet confidence grounded in her actual strengths and values, while acknowledging areas for growth. Within weeks, the first leader was struggling with resistance and credibility challenges, while the second had established genuine influence and respect.

The principle revealed through this contrast is powerful. Sustainable authority flows from authentic leadership aligned with organizational context. Your goal on day one isn't to perform authority but to express it through your genuine strengths, values, and leadership approach. The confidence that comes from being your best authentic self is both more sustainable and more influential than any leadership persona you might adopt.

Remember, day-one authority isn't about dominance or control. It's about establishing yourself as a leader worth following, a partner worth engaging, and a professional worth respecting. By approaching this critical day with strategic intent, you set the foundation for sustainable leadership influence.

WRITING YOUR LEADERSHIP OPENING CHAPTER

As we conclude this chapter, remember that day one represents the opening scene in your leadership story. The impressions you create, the expectations you establish, and the connections you begin forming will ripple throughout your leadership tenure. By approaching this day with strategic intent rather than passive participation, you take control of your leadership narrative from the very beginning.

The confidence and authority you establish on day one isn't just about making a good impression. It's about creating momentum that will carry you through the inevitable challenges of your first 90 days. When you demonstrate confident, authentic leadership from the start, you create a positive expectation that becomes self-reinforcing. People begin looking for evidence that confirms their initial positive impression rather than seeking reasons to doubt your capability.

Your preparation for day one reflects a fundamental leadership truth. Extraordinary results begin with extraordinary beginnings. The HR leaders who create the greatest organizational impact don't leave their initial leadership positioning to chance. They approach it with the same strategic thinking they bring to major HR initiatives.

As you prepare to write the opening chapter of your HR leadership story, commit to showing up as your most confident, authentic, and prepared self. Develop your knowledge foundation, craft your key messages, plan your strategic interactions, and practice the presence that conveys both confidence and approachability.

Your leadership story awaits its opening chapter. How compelling will you make it?

CHAPTER 5:
EMOTIONAL INTELLIGENCE IN HR LEADERSHIP

THE HEART OF STRATEGIC HR LEADERSHIP

"Technical expertise gets you hired. Emotional intelligence gets you promoted, but only the masterful blend of both makes you an extraordinary HR leader."

The most sophisticated HR strategy, meticulously designed compensation structure, or cutting-edge talent acquisition approach will ultimately fail without one critical element—the emotional intelligence to implement it effectively. While technical HR knowledge forms the foundation of your professional capability, emotional intelligence impacts your leadership ceiling.

For HR leaders specifically, emotional intelligence isn't merely an enhancement to effectiveness. It's a fundamental prerequisite for success. As the function responsible for navigating the most complex human dynamics in the organization, HR is under constant evaluation for its own demonstration of interpersonal excellence. The credibility gap that emerges when HR leaders prescribe emotional intelligence competencies they themselves don't display undermines both personal and functional effectiveness.

Despite its critical importance, emotional intelligence remains misunderstood and underdeveloped in many HR leaders. Some mistakenly equate it with simply being nice or agreeable, missing its deeper strategic dimensions. Others view it as an innate trait rather than a set of skills that can be systematically developed. Too many fail to recognize how emotional intelligence specifically manifests in the unique challenges HR leaders face.

The harsh reality is that even the most technically proficient HR leaders hit career ceilings when they lack emotional intelligence, but when technical expertise and emotional intelligence are integrated, HR leaders create distinctive value that elevates both their function and their career trajectory. The journey to this integration begins with understanding what emotional intelligence truly means in the HR leadership context.

Contrary to popular belief, emotional intelligence is not a fixed trait. It is a set of capabilities that can be systematically developed. The key is approaching this development with the same structured intentionality you would bring to technical skill building.

THE EMOTIONAL INTELLIGENCE AWAKENING

Early in my HR leadership journey, I learned a painful lesson about the true nature of emotional intelligence and its impact on leadership effectiveness. This experience fundamentally shifted my understanding of what makes an exceptional HR leader.

I was leading a complex organizational restructuring that required significant changes to long-established teams. My technical approach was flawless. I had meticulously analyzed spans of control, reporting relationships, and skill distributions. The new structure was logically sound and aligned with business objectives. I had prepared detailed documentation, transition plans, and communication materials. From a purely technical perspective, it was exemplary HR work.

However, when the implementation began, I encountered unexpected resistance that threatened the entire initiative. Even leaders who had initially supported the concept began expressing concerns and hesitations. The confusion and frustration I felt quickly turned to defensiveness. I had done everything "right" according to my technical expertise, so why weren't people responding rationally to this clearly superior organizational design?

In a moment of frustration after a particularly difficult meeting, a trusted mentor asked me a question that stopped me cold. They asked, "You've thought deeply about the structural logic of this reorganization, but have you considered its emotional logic?"

This question catalyzed a profound realization. I had approached the restructuring as a technical exercise rather than a human experience. I hadn't adequately recognized the psychological impact of breaking established teams, the identity threat some leaders felt when their spans of control changed, or the anxiety generated by uncertainty, even when the end state was objectively better.

I immediately shifted my approach. Rather than continuing to explain the technical merits of the new structure, I began creating spaces for people to express their concerns. I acknowledged the emotional dimensions of the change rather than just its rational benefits. I adjusted implementation timelines to allow for psychological adjustments alongside the structural transition.

The initiative's trajectory changed dramatically. What had been heading toward failure gradually gained momentum as people felt heard, and they felt that their emotional responses were validated. The final structure remained largely as I had originally designed it, but the path to implementation incorporated the human experience in ways my initial approach had neglected.

This experience taught me that emotional intelligence in HR leadership isn't about abandoning analytical rigor or technical excellence. It's about integrating emotional awareness with technical expertise to create solutions that work in the real human environment of organizations. True emotional intelligence doesn't replace rational analysis; it complements and completes it.

THE FOUR DIMENSIONS OF HR EMOTIONAL INTELLIGENCE

Emotional intelligence in HR leadership encompasses four interconnected dimensions, each with specific relevance to the unique challenges HR leaders face:

1. **Self-Awareness**: Understanding your own emotional patterns, triggers, and impact

2. **Self-Management**: Regulating your emotions and behaviors in service of leadership effectiveness

3. **Social Awareness**: Perceiving and interpreting others' emotions and organizational emotional dynamics

4. **Relationship Management**: Using emotional understanding to build influence and navigate complex interactions

Let's explore each dimension and its specific application to HR leadership challenges.

Self-Awareness: The Foundation of HR Emotional Intelligence

Self-awareness functions as the cornerstone of emotional intelligence for HR leaders. Without clear insight into your own emotional patterns, you cannot effectively navigate the complex human dynamics inherent in HR leadership.

The HR Self-Awareness Challenge

HR leaders face unique self-awareness challenges. As the function responsible for addressing others' emotional and interpersonal challenges, HR professionals often develop sophisticated mechanisms for focusing externally while neglecting internal emotional awareness. Additionally, the expectation that HR should model ideal emotional behavior can create pressure to suppress authentic emotional responses, further disconnecting HR leaders from their own emotional reality.

Self-Management: Emotional Regulation for HR Effectiveness

Self-management builds on self-awareness by focusing on how HR leaders regulate and channel their emotions for maximum leadership effectiveness. This dimension is particularly crucial given the emotionally charged nature of many HR responsibilities.

The HR Self-Management Challenge

HR leaders routinely face situations that generate strong emotional responses: delivering difficult feedback, navigating organizational politics, implementing unpopular decisions, or balancing competing stakeholder needs. The function's position at the intersection of business imperatives and human impacts creates unique emotional regulation challenges.

Social Awareness: Reading the Human Landscape

Social awareness encompasses the ability to accurately perceive and interpret the emotions of others and the broader emotional dynamics within the organization. For HR leaders, this dimension functions as a critical strategic input rather than merely a social skill.

The HR Social Awareness Challenge

HR leaders must navigate complex emotional landscapes that include both explicit and implicit dimensions. The political sensitivity of many HR issues means that stated positions often differ from underlying emotional realities. Additionally, HR's formal role sometimes creates barriers to authentic emotional expression from others, requiring heightened perceptiveness.

Relationship Management: The Currency of HR Influence

Relationship management leverages self-awareness, self-management, and social awareness to build and maintain effective relationships that enable HR leadership influence. For HR leaders who often must lead through influence rather than direct authority, this dimension is particularly critical.

The HR Relationship Management Challenge

HR leaders face unique relationship challenges, including being perceived as policy enforcers rather than strategic partners, navigating dual loyalties to employees and the organization, and building trusting relationships while sometimes delivering difficult messages or decisions.

EMOTIONAL INTELLIGENCE AS COMPETITIVE ADVANTAGE

As we conclude this chapter, it's important to recognize that emotional intelligence isn't merely a "soft skill" enhancement to your HR leadership. It's a fundamental competitive advantage in today's complex organizational environment. As technical HR knowledge becomes increasingly accessible and standardized, emotional intelligence becomes the critical differentiator between average and exceptional HR leaders.

Your investment in emotional intelligence development isn't separate from your development as an HR leader. It's integral to it. The capabilities we've explored in this chapter directly impact your ability to implement the strategies covered throughout this book. Without emotional intelligence, your onboarding plan, learning acceleration, day-one authority, and other leadership dimensions will fall short of their potential.

The intersection of technical HR expertise and emotional intelligence creates a leadership capability that is both rare and increasingly valuable. By developing both dimensions simultaneously, you position yourself not just for success in your current role but for sustainable career advancement as an HR leader who creates distinctive value.

Will you approach emotional intelligence as a fundamental leadership capability or merely a nice-to-have enhancement? The answer to this question may well determine your ultimate ceiling as an HR leader.

CHAPTER 6:
MANAGING TEAM DYNAMICS AND KEY RELATIONSHIPS

THE RELATIONAL ARCHITECTURE OF LEADERSHIP SUCCESS

"Technical knowledge makes you competent. Emotional intelligence makes you effective, but relationship mastery makes you indispensable."

The most brilliant HR strategy, meticulously crafted with perfect technical expertise and delivered with impeccable emotional intelligence, will ultimately fail without one critical element—the relationships required to translate your vision into reality. While your knowledge and capabilities form your leadership foundation, your relationships determine your ability to mobilize those capabilities for organizational impact.

For HR leaders specifically, relationship mastery operates at two distinct but interconnected levels. First, you must build and manage the internal dynamics of your HR team, transforming a collection of HR professionals into a cohesive, high-performing unit. Second, you must establish strategic relationships across the organization that create the influence pathways necessary for HR effectiveness. Excellence at either level without the other creates a fundamental leadership limitation.

Many new HR leaders underestimate the strategic importance of these relational dimensions. Some focus exclusively on HR program development while neglecting team culture. Others invest heavily in executive relationships while failing to build the team capability required to deliver on commitments, and too many leaders approach relationships reactively, responding to immediate needs rather than strategically architecting their relationship ecosystem.

This chapter explores the critical intersection of team dynamics and strategic relationships that determines HR leadership effectiveness. We'll examine what distinguishes high-performing HR teams from merely functional ones, why certain relationships disproportionately impact your leadership success, and how you can systematically develop both dimensions during your critical first 90 days and beyond. You'll learn specific strategies for assessing team dynamics, building team cohesion, identifying key relationship priorities, and establishing influence through strategic relationship investment.

The reality of modern organizations is undeniable. No HR leader succeeds alone. Your effectiveness will be multiplied or constrained by the quality of your team and the strength of your relationships. The question isn't whether these dimensions matter. It's whether you'll approach them with the same strategic intention you bring to other leadership responsibilities.

THE TEAM TRANSFORMATION CHALLENGE

Early in my HR leadership journey, I inherited a team that fundamentally altered my understanding of team dynamics and their impact on leadership effectiveness. This experience crystallized principles that have guided my approach to team leadership ever since.

The team I inherited appeared functional on the surface. HR processes were generally executed on time. Basic services were delivered, and no major compliance issues existed, yet something was clearly missing. The team operated as a collection of individual contributors rather than a cohesive unit. Each person managed their specific responsibility with little collaboration or collective ownership. Knowledge was siloed. Innovation was minimal, and the group's impact was far less than the sum of its individual talents. The executive director led her team of directors one way, and her directors led their teams another way. A great team consisted of four HR functions, and they all were siloed.

Most concerning was the team's reputation within the organization. Rather than being viewed as strategic partners, they were seen as transactional processors—necessary but not particularly valuable beyond basic HR administration. This perception severely limited HR's influence on important organizational decisions.

I initially approached this challenge with a programmatic mindset, focusing on restructuring responsibilities, clarifying goals, and improving processes. While these technical changes were necessary, they produced minimal impact on the team's effectiveness and reputation. The fundamental issue wasn't structural. It was relational.

This realization led me to shift my approach entirely. Instead of continuing to focus on what the team did, I began focusing on how they worked together. I initiated a series of candid conversations about team identity, collaboration barriers, and collective aspirations. We examined unhealthy team patterns, established new norms for interaction, and created shared ownership for our team's organizational impact.

The transformation was remarkable. Within three months, the energy and output of the team had visibly shifted. Collaboration replaced isolation. Innovation emerged naturally, and team members began proactively supporting each other rather than focusing solely on individual responsibilities. Most importantly, the team's organizational reputation began to evolve as others experienced their new collective capability.

This experience taught me that team dynamics aren't just a leadership "nice-to-have." They are a fundamental performance driver that can elevate or undermine everything else you do as an HR leader. A technically skilled team without cohesion will always deliver less value than one with both technical capability and strong relational dynamics. For access to a high performing team blueprint, visit www.Drsheilagilbert.com. There you can also find the 14 Day Team Engagement Challenge blueprint.

THE FIVE DIMENSIONS OF HIGH-PERFORMING HR TEAMS

Through both research and experience leading multiple HR teams, I've identified five critical dimensions that distinguish truly high-performing HR teams from merely functional ones:

1. **Shared Purpose**: A compelling common understanding of the team's unique value contribution

2. **Psychological Safety**: An environment where risk-taking, vulnerability, and challenging the status quo are encouraged

3. **Collaborative Capability**: The skills and structures needed for effective cross-functional integration

4. **Healthy Conflict Management**: The ability to engage disagreement productively rather than destructively

5. **Mutual Accountability**: Collective ownership for team outcomes beyond individual responsibilities

Let's explore each dimension with specific strategies for development.

Shared Purpose: The Foundation of Team Cohesion

Shared purpose provides the gravitational center that transforms individual HR professionals into a cohesive team with collective impact. Without this foundation, technical excellence simply creates a group of skilled individuals rather than a true team.

The HR Shared Purpose Challenge

HR teams face unique challenges in establishing shared purpose. The breadth of HR responsibilities—from compliance to talent development to strategic partnership—can create fragmentation without a unifying purpose. Additionally, HR professionals often identify more strongly with their specific expertise area (compensation, learning and development, talent acquisition) than with the HR function as a whole.

Strategies for Building HR Team Shared Purpose

Purpose Articulation: Develop a clear, compelling statement that defines why your HR team exists beyond administrative functions, connecting your work to meaningful organizational impact; collaboratively draft this statement with team input and refine it until it resonates with all members.

Purpose Reinforcement: Consistently integrate your team's purpose into daily operations through dedicated time in meetings to share purpose-aligned wins and recognize team members who exemplify purpose-driven behaviors; create visual reminders in workspaces and establish regular reflection sessions where team members share how their work connected to the larger purpose.

Purpose Evolution: Establish a regular cadence (quarterly or semi-annually) to revisit and refine your team's purpose based on changing organizational needs and feedback; collect data on how effectively the current purpose statement guides decision-making and motivates the team and make collaborative adjustments as needed.

Psychological Safety: The Catalyst for Excellence

Psychological safety—the shared belief that team members can take interpersonal risks without fear of negative consequences—functions as the critical enabler for team learning, innovation, and adaptation. Research consistently demonstrates that psychological safety is the most significant predictor of team effectiveness.

The HR Psychological Safety Challenge

HR teams encounter unique psychological safety challenges. As the function responsible for performance management and policy enforcement, HR professionals often develop heightened caution about making mistakes or appearing uncertain. Additionally, HR's professional emphasis on confidentiality can unintentionally create communication barriers within the team itself.

Strategies for Building HR Team Psychological Safety

Leadership Modeling: Demonstrate vulnerability by openly admitting mistakes and showing that thoughtful risk-taking is valued; share your own learning experiences in team meetings and respond constructively when team members voice concerns or new ideas.

Norm Establishment: Create explicit team agreements about communication, feedback, and decision-making that prioritize respect and inclusion; collaboratively develop and document these norms and regularly revisit them during team check-ins.

Trust-Building Rituals: Design structured opportunities for team members to connect personally and develop mutual understanding; incorporate brief personal check-ins at the start of meetings and schedule occasional informal gatherings with activities that reveal each person's strengths and perspectives.

Safety Monitoring: Regularly assess psychological safety levels through anonymous surveys and observation of team dynamics; track key indicators like speaking time distribution in meetings and idea contribution rates across team members and conduct periodic pulse checks on comfort levels while allowing others to express divergent viewpoints.

Collaborative Capability: The Integration Advantage

Collaborative capability encompasses the team's ability to work across functional boundaries, integrate diverse expertise, and create collective output greater than what individuals could produce separately. This capability is particularly crucial for HR teams given the interdependent nature of HR specialties.

The HR Collaboration Challenge

HR teams frequently struggle with true collaboration despite their relational focus. The specialized nature of HR expertise—with compensation, talent acquisition, employee relations, and other areas requiring distinct knowledge—can create functional silos that impede integration. Additionally, the high workload many HR teams carry creates pressure to focus exclusively on individual responsibilities at the expense of collaboration.

Strategies for Building HR Team Collaborative Capability

Structural Integration: Create formal connections between HR team activities and organizational processes to ensure HR initiatives directly support business outcomes; establish regular cross-functional meetings with department leaders and map HR deliverables to specific business objectives.

Process Facilitation: Design and manage structured interactions that enable effective collaboration and decision-making within the HR team and across departments; train team members in facilitation techniques and assign facilitation roles for key initiatives based on individual strengths.

Skill Development: Identify and systematically build both technical and interpersonal capabilities needed for HR excellence in your specific organizational context; create personalized learning plans for each team member and allocate protected time for skill practice and knowledge sharing.

Recognition Alignment: Ensure that the ways team members are acknowledged and rewarded directly reinforce behaviors that advance organizational goals and team purpose; establish clear criteria for recognition tied to purpose-driven outcomes and create regular opportunities to celebrate contributions that exemplify these standards.

Healthy Conflict Management: The Productive Tension

Healthy conflict management enables teams to leverage different perspectives for better outcomes rather than suppress disagreement or allow it to become personal. For HR teams, this capability is both particularly important and especially challenging.

The HR Conflict Management Challenge

HR teams face a distinctive conflict management paradox. As the function that often helps others navigate workplace conflict, HR professionals can develop conflict-avoidant cultures within their own teams. The desire to model ideal workplace behavior can create pressure to maintain surface harmony at the expense of encouraging productive disagreements about important issues.

Strategies for Building HR Team Conflict Management Capacity

Conflict Reframing: Transform how team members perceive disagreement by explicitly positioning it as a valuable source of innovation and clarity rather than a problem to avoid; highlight examples where differing perspectives lead to better outcomes and use language that emphasizes "exploration of different viewpoints" rather than "conflict resolution."

Productive Debate Structures: Create formal frameworks that guide how the team discusses contentious issues to maximize learning while minimizing interpersonal friction; establish specific meeting formats with clear roles (like devil's advocate), time boundaries, and decision-making protocols that separate idea generation from evaluation.

Dialogue Skill Building: Develop team members' abilities to engage in difficult conversations with curiosity and respect rather than defensiveness; provide training in specific techniques like asking genuine questions, paraphrasing others' perspectives, and expressing disagreement in ways that focus on issues rather than individuals.

Conflict Intervention Protocols: Establish clear processes for addressing conflicts that have become unproductive or personally hurtful; create tiered response guidelines that outline when peer mediation is appropriate versus when leadership intervention is needed and train select team members in basic mediation techniques.

Mutual accountability creates collective ownership for team outcomes rather than responsibility limited to individual areas. This capability transforms HR from a collection of specialists into a true team with a shared commitment to overall effectiveness.

The HR Mutual Accountability Challenge

The specialized nature of HR expertise creates natural boundaries that can impede mutual accountability. When team members focus exclusively on their functional excellence—whether in talent acquisition, compensation, employee relations, or other HR specialties—collective ownership for HR's overall impact can diminish. Additionally, the confidential nature of some HR work can create information asymmetries that make mutual support challenging.

Strategies for Building HR Team Mutual Accountability

- Shift accountability from activities to outcomes.
- Build awareness of how team members depend on each other.
- Implement systems that enable team members to support each other.
- Establish processes for addressing performance gaps as a team.

STRATEGIC RELATIONSHIP MANAGEMENT: BEYOND THE HR TEAM

While internal team dynamics form the foundation of your leadership effectiveness, your impact as an HR leader ultimately depends on your ability to build and leverage strategic relationships across the organization. These relationships create the influence pathways required to implement HR initiatives and drive organizational change.

Key Relationship Categories for HR Leaders

Effective HR leaders strategically develop relationships across four critical categories:

1. **Executive Stakeholders**: Senior leaders whose decision-making authority directly impacts HR effectiveness

2. **Operational Partners**: Mid-level managers who translate HR initiatives into front-line implementation

3. **Influence Multipliers**: Informal leaders whose support amplifies HR impact regardless of formal position

4. **Professional Resources**: Internal and external experts who provide specialized knowledge or support

Each category requires a distinct relationship development approach aligned with both organizational needs and individual stakeholder characteristics.

Executive Stakeholder Relationship Development

Relationships with executive stakeholders create the strategic foundation for HR effectiveness. These relationships determine your ability to influence key decisions, secure necessary resources, and align HR initiatives with organizational priorities.

The Executive Relationship Challenge

Building effective executive relationships presents unique challenges for HR leaders. The historical perception of HR as primarily administrative rather than strategic can create credibility barriers. Additionally, executive stakeholders often have limited time and attention, requiring highly focused relationship development approaches.

In today's fast-paced business world, aligning HR strategies with executive priorities can be the key to establishing strong, influential relationships with top leadership. By mastering the art of understanding executives' needs, tailoring communication, and providing value-driven interactions, HR leaders can build a lasting and powerful connection with their stakeholders.

Here's a streamlined guide to help you build and nurture these executive relationships:

1. **Strategic Value Alignment**

   - **Connect with Executives Through Their Specific Priorities**

     Understand the key business objectives and challenges of each executive. Identify how HR initiatives support their goals and frame your approach in terms of their specific needs, demonstrating your business acumen to earn credibility.

2. **Communication Customization**

   - **Tailor Your Communication Approach**

     Adapt your communication to each executive's preferences—whether they prefer detailed data or high-level summaries. Respect their time by being outcome-focused and build regular communication rhythms that suit their availability and decision-making style.

3. Value-Based Visibility

- **Create Visibility Through Value Contribution**

  Instead of simply being present, ensure your contributions are meaningful. Identify ways to add value in executive forums, always linking HR initiatives to strategic business priorities. Follow through on your commitments to establish your reliability and credibility.

4. Relationship Investment Beyond Transactions

- **Develop Relationship Depth**

  Go beyond immediate HR needs and show a genuine interest in the executive's leadership challenges. Offer support that transcends HR responsibilities. Share insights without expecting anything in return and identify personal connection points to build stronger relationships.

Mastering these steps to building executive relationships isn't just about HR showing up. It's about making sure HR adds value in every interaction. By aligning your HR efforts with strategic priorities, customizing your communication, and fostering genuine connections, you'll not only gain trust, but you will also become a key partner in your organization's leadership team. The result is a relationship that's built to last and deliver exceptional results.

OPERATIONAL PARTNER RELATIONSHIP DEVELOPMENT

While executive relationships provide strategic direction, operational partner relationships determine implementation effectiveness. These mid-level leaders translate HR initiatives into practical application and provide the ground-level feedback essential for program refinement.

The Operational Relationship Challenge

HR leaders often struggle with operational relationships for several reasons. Mid-level managers frequently view HR initiatives as compliance requirements that compete with operational priorities rather than enabling tools. Additionally, these leaders often have significant informal influence that can either accelerate or undermine HR effectiveness.

The strategies below create a clear path for cultivating strong operational partnerships:

1. **Implementation Partnership**

   - **Position HR as an Implementation Partner**

     Involve operational leaders early in HR initiatives, seeking their input on potential challenges. Co-create solutions that address both HR requirements and operational needs while maintaining a flexible approach focused on outcomes.

2. **Value Demonstration**

   - **Consistently Demonstrate HR's Value to Operational Priorities**

     Align HR programs directly with operational performance metrics. Provide practical tools and resources, not just abstract policies. Be responsive to urgent needs and share data that supports operational decision-making to demonstrate HR's impact.

3. Accessibility Enhancement

- **Create Multiple Avenues for Engagement**

  Set up regular touchpoints beyond formal meetings and ensure quick responses to pressing issues. Make HR expertise and resources easily accessible and actively engage in operational environments rather than expecting leaders to seek you out.

4. Recognition and Advocacy

- **Become an Advocate for Operational Leaders**

  Recognize and celebrate the contributions of operational leaders in implementing HR initiatives. Amplify their insights in relevant forums and advocate for their needs with executive leadership, giving credit where it's due to strengthen collaboration.

Successful operational partnerships require HR to move beyond being a policy enforcer to become a proactive, solution-oriented partner. By consistently demonstrating value, being accessible, and advocating for operational leaders, HR can build partnerships that drive performance and align both HR and operational goals. This mutual collaboration isn't just about implementing initiatives. It's about creating a shared success story.

INFLUENCE MULTIPLIER RELATIONSHIP DEVELOPMENT

Beyond formal leadership positions, every organization contains informal influence multipliers—individuals whose support or resistance disproportionately impacts initiative success regardless of their position. Identifying and engaging these multipliers is crucial for HR effectiveness.

The Influence Multiplier Challenge

HR leaders face several challenges in developing relationships with influence multipliers. These individuals are often difficult to identify through organizational charts alone, requiring cultural understanding and network analysis. Additionally, their informal influence means traditional authority-based approaches are ineffective for relationship development.

Here's how to build relationships with influence multipliers and make them your strongest allies:

1. Multiplier Identification

- **Systematically Identify Key Influence Multipliers**

    Pay attention to individuals whose opinions are frequently sought after in discussions and those who can shift group perspectives with their comments. Recognize people with broad relationship networks and those who hold "cultural credibility" beyond their formal role.

2. Authentic Engagement

- **Develop Relationships Based on Genuine Value Exchange**

   Engage with influence multipliers by showing authentic interest in their perspectives. Seek their input early in your initiatives and share the context behind decisions. Build connections grounded in shared values, not just transactional needs.

3. Insight Sharing

- **Create Mutual Value Through Information Exchange**

   Share relevant organizational insights with influence multipliers within appropriate boundaries. Offer HR expertise that helps them address their own challenges, and connect them to valuable resources or relationships. Provide early visibility into changes that may impact their areas of responsibility.

4. Strategic Involvement

- **Involve Influence Multipliers in Ways That Leverage Their Informal Impact**

   Include them in early pilot programs or feedback groups and invite their participation in initiative design, not just during implementation. Create ambassador roles that formalize their informal influence and develop their capabilities as change agents for key initiatives.

Building relationships with influence multipliers is one of the most powerful ways to extend your impact across the organization. By identifying key individuals, engaging with them authentically, and strategically involving them in your initiatives, you can create a ripple effect of influence that leads to greater success and momentum. When you empower these multipliers, you multiply your influence, transforming your initiatives into organization-wide achievements.

PROFESSIONAL RESOURCE RELATIONSHIP DEVELOPMENT

The final relationship category encompasses the professional resources—both internal and external—who provide specialized expertise, perspective, and support for your HR leadership. These relationships extend your capability beyond your personal knowledge and your team's capacity.

The Professional Resource Challenge

HR leaders often underinvest in professional resource relationships for several reasons. The pressure to demonstrate self-sufficiency can create reluctance to seek external support. Additionally, the breadth of HR responsibilities makes it challenging to develop deep relationships across all potentially relevant resource domains.

Here's a practical guide to building and managing professional resource relationships:

1. Resource Network Mapping

- **Identify the Full Spectrum of Potential Professional Resources**

  Map out key internal subject matter experts beyond HR as well as external consultants with specialized expertise. Engage with professional associations, networks, and thought leaders in relevant domains to build a robust resource network that extends beyond your immediate team.

2. Value Exchange Cultivation

- **Build Relationships Based on Mutual Value Creation**

  Share organizational insights with your resources and offer them opportunities to showcase their expertise. Build relationships grounded in mutual benefit by connecting them with valuable contacts, providing meaningful feedback, and fostering collaboration.

Strategic Engagement Planning

- **Develop Intentional Approaches to Resource Engagement**

  Identify specific gaps where external expertise is needed and create structured mechanisms for knowledge transfer. Establish clear parameters for each resource relationship to ensure both parties benefit and build regular connection points to keep relationships strong as needs evolve.

3. Integration Management

- **Effectively Integrate External Resources Into Your Leadership Approach**

    Establish clear roles, expectations, and protocols for engaging external resources. Ensure knowledge-sharing between resources and your team, maintain leadership authority with appropriate boundaries, and develop transition plans that sustain value beyond individual engagements.

Building professional resource relationships is not just about accessing expertise. It's about creating an ecosystem where resources, both internal and external, are integrated seamlessly into your leadership efforts. By strategically mapping your resources, fostering value-based relationships, and planning for integration, you can elevate your leadership approach and consistently address challenges with the best support available. When done right, these relationships become a cornerstone of sustainable leadership success.

THE RELATIONSHIP ARCHITECT: YOUR LEADERSHIP DIFFERENTIATOR

As we conclude this chapter, it's essential to recognize that your ability to architect and develop a high-functioning relationship ecosystem—both within your team and across the organization—represents perhaps your greatest leadership differentiator as an HR leader. While technical HR knowledge is increasingly accessible and commoditized, the ability to build and leverage relationship systems remains a distinctive capability that directly impacts organizational effectiveness.

The HR leaders who create the greatest impact aren't just technically proficient or even emotionally intelligent. They're skilled relationship architects who systematically develop both internal team dynamics and external influence networks. They recognize that relationships aren't peripheral to HR leadership. They're the primary medium through which HR creates organizational value.

Your investment in relationship ecosystem development isn't separate from your development as an HR leader. It's integral to it. The strategies we've explored in this chapter directly impact your ability to implement the technical aspects of HR leadership covered throughout this book. Without effective team dynamics and strategic relationships, even the most sophisticated HR approaches will struggle to gain traction.

As you continue your HR leadership journey, commit to developing your relationship ecosystem with the same strategic intention you bring to developing HR programs and policies. Regularly assess both team dynamics and key relationships, identify development priorities in both dimensions, and create integrated approaches that build your overall relationship capability.

The intersection of strong team dynamics and strategic external relationships creates a leadership foundation that enables sustainable impact far beyond what technical expertise alone can achieve. By developing both dimensions simultaneously, you position yourself not just for success in your current role but for expanding influence as an HR leader who creates distinctive organizational value.

Will you approach relationship development as a strategic leadership priority or merely as a nice-to-have addition to technical excellence? Your answer to this question will likely determine the ultimate ceiling of your HR leadership impact.

CHAPTER 7:
SETTING AND CLARIFYING EXPECTATIONS

THE EXPECTATIONS PARADOX

"In HR leadership, unspoken expectations are unmet expectations. The conversations you avoid today become the crises you manage tomorrow."

The most meticulously crafted HR strategy, built with impeccable technical expertise, supported by emotional intelligence, and implemented through strong relationships, will ultimately fail without one critical element—crystal clear expectations. While your knowledge, capabilities, and relationships form the engine of your leadership, expectations provide the roadmap that determines your destination.

For HR leaders specifically, expectations operate as both a leadership tool and a potential liability. As the function responsible for performance management processes and leadership development, HR is held to a higher standard for expectation clarity than perhaps any other organizational function. The credibility gap that emerges when HR leaders fail to masterfully manage expectations in their own domain undermines both personal and functional effectiveness.

However, expectations remain one of the most chronically mismanaged dimensions of HR leadership. Some leaders avoid explicit expectation discussions entirely, assuming shared understanding that rarely exists. Others establish initial expectations but fail to recalibrate as circumstances evolve, and many focus exclusively on downward expectations—what they expect from others—

while neglecting upward and lateral expectation alignment that ultimately determines their success.

This chapter explores the critical importance of expectation management in HR leadership effectiveness. We'll examine why misaligned expectations create the root cause of most leadership derailments, how expectation dynamics shift during your first 90 days, and how you can systematically develop expectation mastery that prevents downstream conflicts. You'll learn specific strategies for establishing, clarifying, negotiating, and evolving expectations across multiple stakeholder relationships.

The uncomfortable reality is that even the most technically brilliant HR leader with strong emotional intelligence and solid relationships will struggle without mastery of expectations. When expectations remain unspoken, they become invisible tripwires that eventually disrupt even the most promising leadership trajectory. The question isn't whether expectations matter. It's whether you'll manage them with the same strategic intention you bring to other leadership dimensions.

THE EXPECTATION ALIGNMENT WAKE-UP CALL

Early in my HR leadership journey, I learned a valuable lesson about expectation alignment that reshaped my approach to leadership. This experience showed me that strong relationships and technical expertise can't overcome misaligned expectations.

I was hired to lead HR at a growing roofing company with a goal to "professionalize" the function. In my interviews with the CEO and team, we discussed the need for better talent systems, compliance processes, and HR strategy. The conversations felt aligned, and I was confident in my ability to deliver.

In the first three months, I focused on technical improvements: implementing a structured performance management process, developing a compensation framework, and creating talent review protocols. My team and I worked hard, and I felt we were making good progress.

However, six months in, I had a surprising conversation with the CEO. He acknowledged the technical improvements, but he was disappointed in my overall impact. He criticized my focus on HR systems instead of culture development, questioned why I wasn't more visible with front-line managers, and expressed concern that I was building an "HR bureaucracy."

I left the meeting confused and unsure why my work had missed the mark. It wasn't until I had a conversation with a trusted colleague that I understood. My colleague said, "You've been following the exact instructions, but not meeting the actual expectations".

That insight helped me realize that the CEO and I had never truly aligned on expectations. When he said "professionalize HR," he meant making HR more accessible and business-focused, while I had interpreted it as building sophisticated systems. We had been on different pages without realizing it.

This experience taught me that expectation alignment isn't automatic. It requires clear communication, exploration, and constant recalibration. I learned that expectations go beyond formal goals to include unspoken assumptions about approach, style, and success.

THE THREE DIMENSIONS OF EXPECTATION MASTERY

Three key dimensions of expectation mastery that are essential to HR leadership effectiveness:

1. **Expectation Discovery**: Systematically uncovering both explicit and implicit expectations across key stakeholder relationships

2. **Expectation Negotiation**: Actively shaping realistic expectations rather than passively accepting impossible demands

3. **Expectation Evolution**: Continuously recalibrating expectations as circumstances, priorities, and capabilities change

Let's explore each dimension with specific strategies for development.

EXPECTATION DISCOVERY: UNCOVERING THE FULL EXPECTATION LANDSCAPE

Expectation discovery focuses on comprehensively understanding what others expect from you and your HR function—not just the formally stated objectives but the full spectrum of explicit and implicit expectations that will determine perceived success.

The HR Expectation Discovery Challenge

HR leaders face unique challenges in expectation discovery. The function's broad mandate creates multiple expectation sources—from executive leaders who want strategic partnership to managers who need operational support to employees who expect advocacy. Additionally, HR's historical reputation in an organization often creates unstated assumptions about what the function should and shouldn't do.

Before acting, you must clearly understand the expectations.

EXPECTATION NEGOTIATION: SHAPING REALISTIC PARAMETERS

Expectation negotiation focuses on actively shaping expectations rather than passively accepting them. This dimension recognizes that not all expectations are realistic or appropriate, and leadership effectiveness requires the courage to negotiate sustainable expectations.

The HR Expectation Negotiation Challenge

HR leaders face several unique negotiation challenges. The function's support orientation can create reluctance to push back on unrealistic expectations. Additionally, the desire to demonstrate strategic value can lead to accepting impossible expectations in an effort to prove HR's worth. This challenge is magnified for new HR leaders eager to establish credibility. This failed approach often can have a detrimental effect on the leader and the function.

EXPECTATION EVOLUTION: NAVIGATING THE CHANGING LANDSCAPE

Expectation evolution focuses on the ongoing recalibration of expectations in response to changing circumstances, emerging information, and evolving priorities. This dimension recognizes that expectations aren't static agreements but dynamic understandings that require continuous adjustment.

The HR Expectation Evolution Challenge

HR leaders face particular challenges in expectation evolution. The function's connection to rapidly changing business conditions creates constantly shifting expectations that can be difficult to track. Additionally, the multi-stakeholder nature of HR means that expectation changes in one relationship can create cascading impacts across others.

Action Step: Establish a regular "Expectation Alignment Review" process for your key HR initiatives and relationships. For each, assess current alignment, identify potential drift areas, and develop specific recalibration actions. Implement this review as a standard leadership practice rather than a crisis response.

THE MULTI-DIRECTIONAL EXPECTATION CHALLENGE

In leading the HR function of a major digital transformation involving significant changes to roles, reporting relationships, and required capabilities, I had an epiphany. My team and I had carefully defined clear expectations with executive stakeholders about timeline, scope, and intended outcomes. We had established detailed implementation plans and communication strategies, and I felt confident in our approach.

As implementation progressed, however, unexpected resistance emerged from both middle managers and employees. Despite transparent communication, we encountered significant pushback, passive resistance, and in some cases outright defiance. Progress slowed dramatically, and organizational anxiety increased rather than decreased with each communication effort.

The breakthrough came during a candid conversation with a respected mid-level leader. When I expressed frustration about the resistance, he offered a perspective that transformed my thoughts. He said, "You've been focused exclusively on what the organization should expect from HR during this transformation, but you haven't explored what HR should expect from the organization."

This one sentence catalyzed a fundamental shift in my approach. I initiated a series of "mutual expectation" conversations across the organization. Instead of simply communicating what we expected from others, we explicitly asked what they expected from us during the transformation and what they needed to do to meet our expectations of them. These conversations revealed critical misalignments in support requirements, readiness assumptions, and capacity expectations.

Most importantly, we discovered that we had established clear outcome expectations while neglecting process expectations—how the transformation would be implemented, what involvement people would have, and how disruption would be managed. This omission had created an expectation vacuum that was being filled with worst-case assumptions based on previous negative experiences.

By reframing expectations as mutual commitments rather than unidirectional demands, we transformed the transformation dynamic. We explicitly negotiated what different stakeholders needed to meet our expectations and what they could realistically expect from us. This mutual expectation clarity created the foundation for a genuine partnership rather than compliance-based implementation.

Effective expectation management isn't about establishing what you expect from others or even understanding what others expect from you. It's about creating integrated expectation systems where mutual expectations are aligned across multiple relationships simultaneously. This multi-directional view represents the highest level of expectation mastery.

THE FIVE EXPECTATION CONVERSATIONS EVERY HR LEADER MUST MASTER

Through my work with hundreds of HR leaders, I've identified five critical expectation conversations that disproportionately impact leadership success:

1. The Role Expectation Conversation

Having this conversation early prevents fundamental misalignment about your role purpose. This foundational discussion clarifies expectations about your role beyond formal job descriptions.

2.   **The Resource Expectation Conversation**

This crucial discussion connects outcome expectations to resource realities.

3.   **The Timeline Expectation Conversation**

This specific discussion aligns expectations about when results will be delivered.

4.   **The Decision Authority Expectation Conversation**

This clarifying discussion establishes expectations about decision rights.

5.   **The Support Expectation Conversation**

This mutual discussion clarifies what support HR needs to be successful.

EXPECTATION MASTERY: YOUR LEADERSHIP INSURANCE POLICY

As we conclude this chapter, it's essential to recognize that expectation mastery functions as perhaps your most important leadership insurance policy. When expectations are clearly established, thoughtfully negotiated, and continuously recalibrated, you create a foundation for sustainable success regardless of the specific HR challenges you face.

The HR leaders who create the greatest organizational impact aren't just technically proficient, emotionally intelligent, and relationally skilled—they're expectation masters who establish, negotiate, and manage expectations with the same strategic intention they bring to other leadership dimensions. They recognize that expectations aren't peripheral to leadership effectiveness. They're the invisible force field that either enables or undermines everything else you do.

Your investment in expectation mastery isn't separate from your development as an HR leader. It's integral to it. The strategies we've explored in this chapter directly impact your ability to implement the technical, emotional, and relational aspects of HR leadership covered throughout this book. Without expectation mastery, even the most sophisticated HR approaches will eventually encounter resistance rooted in misaligned expectations.

As you continue your HR leadership journey, commit to developing expectation mastery with the same dedication you bring to building other leadership capabilities. Regularly assess expectation alignment across key relationships, identify emerging expectation gaps before they become problems, and create systems that support ongoing expectation clarity rather than assuming shared understanding.

The intersection of technical expertise, emotional intelligence, relationship mastery, and expectation excellence creates a leadership foundation that enables sustainable impact far beyond what any single dimension can achieve. By developing all dimensions simultaneously, you position yourself not just for success in your current role but for expanding influence as an HR leader who consistently delivers and exceeds the expectations that matter most. A clear expectation blueprint guide can be accessed at www. Drsheilagilbert.com.

Will you treat expectation management as a fundamental leadership capability or merely hope that good intentions will bridge expectation gaps? Your answer to this question may well determine whether your HR leadership journey fulfills its potential or falls short of what's possible.

CHAPTER 8:
PROBLEM-SOLVING AND FOSTERING COLLABORATION

THE COLLABORATIVE PROBLEM-SOLVING ADVANTAGE

> *"Technical solutions without collaboration create compliance. Collaborative solutions create commitment, and only commitment drives sustainable change."*

The most brilliantly designed HR initiative, meticulously researched and technically flawless, will ultimately fail without one critical element—collaborative problem-solving that engages the hearts and minds of those who must implement it. While your expertise and vision form the foundation of your HR leadership, your ability to foster true collaboration determines whether your solutions create temporary compliance or lasting change.

For HR leaders specifically, problem-solving exists at a unique intersection of technical knowledge, business objectives, and human dynamics. Your function is simultaneously expected to solve complex organizational problems while modeling the collaborative approaches that build organizational capability. The credibility gap that emerges when HR leaders prescribe collaboration while practicing isolation undermines both personal and functional effectiveness.

Yet despite its critical importance, collaborative problem-solving remains one of the most underutilized leadership approaches in HR. Some leaders default to technical expertise, developing solutions in isolation and then struggling with implementation resistance. Others mistake consensus-building for collaboration, diluting solutions in an effort to accommodate every perspective. Many fail to recognize how collaborative approaches must be adapted to different organizational problems and contexts.

This chapter explores collaborative problem-solving as the critical differentiator in HR leadership effectiveness. We'll examine what distinguishes true collaboration from mere coordination or consensus, why collaborative approaches are particularly powerful for HR challenges, and how you can systematically develop collaborative problem-solving capability during your critical first 90 days and beyond. You'll learn specific strategies for identifying which problems require collaboration, engaging diverse stakeholders effectively, navigating collaborative tensions productively, and translating collaborative insights into implementable solutions.

The uncomfortable reality is that even the most technically brilliant HR leader will encounter implementation ceiling after implementation ceiling without collaborative problem-solving mastery. When solutions are created in isolation—no matter how expertly designed—they inevitably miss critical context, encounter unexpected resistance, and fail to build the ownership required for sustainable implementation. The question isn't whether collaboration matters. It's whether you'll approach it with the same strategic intention you bring to technical solution development.

THE COLLABORATIVE AWAKENING

My understanding of collaborative problem-solving was fundamentally transformed through a challenging experience early in my HR leadership journey. This painful lesson forever changed my approach to addressing complex organizational problems.

I had been tasked with redesigning our performance management system—a system universally acknowledged as broken. Managers complained about administrative burden. Employees described the process as demotivating rather than developmental, and executives questioned the value of the significant time investment. With my background in talent management and organizational psychology, I was confident in my ability to design a superior alternative.

I immersed myself in research, analyzing best practices and emerging approaches across industries. I consulted academic literature on effective feedback and development. I created a streamlined design that incorporated continuous feedback, reduced documentation requirements, and aligned individual objectives with organizational priorities. From a technical perspective, the solution was elegant and addressed every known issue with the current system.

When I unveiled the new design to our leadership team, I expected enthusiasm and support. Instead, I encountered skepticism, resistance, and a barrage of "yes, but" responses, highlighting potential implementation challenges I hadn't considered. Despite the acknowledged problems with the current system, there was little appetite for implementing my carefully crafted solution.

Frustrated and confused, I sought guidance from a trusted mentor who had successfully led many organizational changes. After listening to my explanation of both the solution and the resistance, she offered an insight that transformed my approach: "You've created a technically sound solution to a problem you understand, but you haven't created a solution to the problem as others experience it, and you've denied them the opportunity to be architects rather than just occupants of the new system."

This perspective catalyzed a complete reset of my approach. Rather than continuing to refine and advocate for my solution, I initiated a collaborative redesign process that engaged stakeholders from across the organization. We established a cross-functional working group that included managers, employees, executives, and HR representatives. Instead of beginning with my solution, we started with collaborative exploration of the current system's challenges from multiple perspectives.

What emerged from this process surprised me. While many of the core features of my original design remained, the collaborative process revealed critical nuances I had missed. Managers identified implementation barriers that weren't visible from my HR perspective. Employees highlighted concerns about fairness and consistency that hadn't appeared in my research. Executives emphasized performance differentiation needs that weren't prominent in my developmental focus.

Most importantly, the collaborative approach transformed ownership. When we eventually rolled out the new system, it wasn't "HR's new performance management process." It was "our new approach to performance and development." The key stakeholders who had participated in its creation became advocates rather than critics, helping address resistance and implementation challenges that inevitably emerged.

This experience taught me that collaborative problem-solving isn't about diluting expertise or seeking lowest-common-denominator solutions. It's about combining technical excellence with diverse perspectives and shared ownership to create solutions that are both technically sound and implementable. Most importantly, I learned that collaboration doesn't just lead to better solutions. It creates the commitment foundation required for successful implementation.

THE THREE DIMENSIONS OF COLLABORATIVE PROBLEM-SOLVING MASTERY

Through both research and experience, I've identified three critical dimensions of collaborative problem-solving that determine HR leadership effectiveness:

1. **Strategic Collaboration Design**: Determining when and how to apply collaborative approaches for maximum impact

2. **Collaborative Process Facilitation**: Effectively guiding diverse stakeholders through productive problem-solving

3. **Collaborative Solution Implementation**: Translating collaborative insights into sustainable organizational change

Let's explore each dimension with specific strategies for development.

STRATEGIC COLLABORATION DESIGN: THE RIGHT APPROACH FOR THE RIGHT PROBLEM

Strategic collaboration design focuses on deliberately structuring collaborative approaches based on problem characteristics rather than defaulting to standard processes. This dimension ensures that collaboration creates value rather than unnecessary complexity or diluted solutions.

The HR Collaboration Design Challenge

HR leaders face unique challenges in collaboration design. The function's position at the intersection of business strategy and employee experience creates pressure to satisfy diverse stakeholders with different priorities. Additionally, the broad scope of HR responsibilities encompasses problems that vary dramatically in complexity, time sensitivity, and implementation requirements, necessitating different collaborative approaches.

Strategies for Strategic Collaboration Design

Develop a systematic approach to categorizing problems based on collaboration requirements.

Create comprehensive maps of potential collaboration participants.

Establish appropriate collaboration levels for different stakeholders.

Design tailored collaborative processes based on problem characteristics.

COLLABORATIVE PROCESS FACILITATION: GUIDING PRODUCTIVE ENGAGEMENT

Collaborative process facilitation focuses on effectively guiding diverse stakeholders through productive problem-solving interactions. This dimension transforms collaboration from unfocused discussion to structured exploration that generates implementable solutions.

The HR Facilitation Challenge

HR leaders encounter unique facilitation challenges due to their dual role as both process guides and content experts. Balancing advocacy for HR perspectives with openness to diverse viewpoints creates an inherent tension. Additionally, facilitating collaboration across organizational levels and functions requires navigating power dynamics, functional biases, and communication differences.

Strategies for Effective Collaborative Facilitation

Create conditions where participants can engage authentically.

Leverage differences as assets rather than obstacles.

Guide the process of combining diverse perspectives into coherent solutions.

Sustain collaborative energy throughout the problem-solving process.

COLLABORATIVE SOLUTION IMPLEMENTATION: FROM INSIGHT TO IMPACT

Collaborative solution implementation focuses on translating collaborative insights into sustainable organizational change. This dimension addresses the common challenge where even effective collaboration fails to generate lasting impact due to implementation breakdowns.

The HR Implementation Challenge

HR leaders face particular challenges in moving from collaborative problem-solving to effective implementation. The function's limited formal authority creates reliance on influence rather than direction. Additionally, HR solutions often require behavior change across multiple organizational levels and functions, creating complex implementation requirements beyond what other functions typically encounter.

THE INTEGRATION CHALLENGE: BALANCING EXPERT AND COLLABORATIVE APPROACHES

My journey with collaborative problem-solving deepened significantly during a complex organizational transformation that required both technical expertise and broad engagement. This experience revealed the sophisticated balance between expert leadership and collaborative engagement that characterizes truly effective HR problem-solving.

The organization was implementing a major digital transformation that required significant changes to roles, skills, and work processes. As HR leader, I was responsible for developing talent strategies that would enable successful transition to the new operating model. The challenge was extraordinarily complex, involving technical workforce planning, skill assessment, learning strategy, and change management considerations.

I initially approached this challenge by assembling a team of HR experts across these domains to develop an integrated talent strategy. We created a comprehensive technical solution that addressed workforce gaps, learning requirements, and transition approaches. The solution was sophisticated and integrated—a testament to the technical expertise of our team.

When we began socializing this approach with organizational leaders, however, we encountered significant resistance despite its technical merits. Leaders questioned our understanding of operational realities, raised concerns about implementation feasibility, and expressed skepticism about adoption potential. Most concerningly, they positioned themselves as recipients rather than owners of the talent strategy, creating significant implementation risk.

This reaction prompted a fundamental reconsideration of our approach. Rather than continuing to refine our expert solution, we restructured the entire problem-solving process. We established a collaborative design approach that engaged leaders from across the organization while preserving our HR technical expertise. Most importantly, we positioned HR's role as providing expertise within a collaborative framework rather than delivering a complete solution for others to implement.

What emerged was a hybrid approach that balanced expert input with collaborative engagement. We created structured collaboration forums where HR provided technical frameworks and options while operational leaders contributed contextual understanding and implementation perspective. Together, we developed integrated solutions that combined HR expertise with operational reality.

The results demonstrated the power of this balanced approach. The technical quality of our talent strategy remained high but with critical refinements that addressed implementation realities we hadn't fully appreciated. Leaders transitioned from skeptics to advocates, actively promoting the approach with their teams. Most importantly, the collaborative process built the shared ownership that ultimately determined implementation success.

This experience taught me that effective HR problem-solving isn't about choosing between expert solutions or collaborative engagement. It's about integrating these approaches in ways that leverage their complementary strengths. The most impactful HR leaders don't abandon their expertise in the name of collaboration; they position that expertise within collaborative frameworks that build both better solutions and deeper commitment.

THE COLLABORATIVE PROBLEM-SOLVING FRAMEWORK: 90-DAY IMPLEMENTATION

I've developed an integrated framework for building collaborative problem-solving capability during your first 90 days as an HR leader:

First 30 Days: Collaboration Foundation

- Assess the current state of collaborative problem-solving within HR and across the organization.

- Identify key stakeholders for potential collaboration on priority challenges.

- Establish initial collaborative processes for immediate HR priorities.

- Model collaborative leadership approaches in your own decision-making.

- Begin building psychological safety for authentic engagement.

Days 31-60: Collaborative Process Development

- Implement structured collaborative approaches for significant HR initiatives.

- Develop facilitation skills for navigating challenging collaborative dynamics.

- Create integration frameworks for combining diverse perspectives.

- Build collaborative networks beyond immediate stakeholders.

- Establish implementation bridges that connect solutions to action.

Days 61-90: Collaborative Capability Expansion

- Extend collaborative problem-solving to complex organizational challenges.

- Develop team capability for facilitating effective collaboration.

- Create sustainable collaborative structures that outlast specific initiatives.

- Establish feedback systems for continuous collaborative improvement.

- Build organizational recognition for collaborative problem-solving value.

This framework ensures progressive development of both personal collaborative capability and organizational collaborative capacity throughout your transition period.

Action Step: Create your "90-Day Collaborative Problem-Solving Plan" using this framework. For each phase, identify specific actions for developing your collaborative leadership approach and building collaborative capability within your HR function and across the organization. Review this plan weekly to assess progress and refine priorities.

COLLABORATIVE PROBLEM-SOLVING: YOUR LEADERSHIP MULTIPLIER

As we conclude this chapter, it's essential to recognize that collaborative problem-solving functions as perhaps your most powerful leadership multiplier as an HR leader. When you master collaborative approaches, you exponentially expand your impact by leveraging diverse expertise, building implementation ownership, and developing organizational capability that extends far beyond your individual capacity.

The HR leaders who create the greatest organizational impact aren't just technically proficient, emotionally intelligent, relationally skilled, expectation-savvy, and learning-agile. They're collaborative masters who engage the full potential of their organizations to address complex challenges. They recognize that collaboration isn't peripheral to leadership effectiveness. It's the fundamental approach that enables sustainable solutions in complex organizational environments.

Your investment in collaborative problem-solving capability isn't separate from your development as an HR leader. It's integral to it. The strategies we've explored in this chapter directly impact your ability to implement the technical, emotional, relational, and learning aspects of HR leadership covered throughout this book. Without collaborative mastery, even the most sophisticated HR approaches will struggle to gain traction beyond limited pockets of the organization.

As you continue your HR leadership journey, commit to developing collaborative problem-solving as a core leadership discipline rather than an occasional approach. Regularly assess your collaborative practices, refine your facilitation skills, and enhance your ability to design tailored collaborative processes. Most importantly, build collaborative capability within your team and across your organization, creating a multiplier effect that extends your leadership influence far beyond your direct actions.

The intersection of technical expertise, emotional intelligence, relationship mastery, expectation clarity, learning velocity, and collaborative excellence creates a leadership foundation that enables sustainable impact far beyond what any single dimension can achieve. By developing all dimensions simultaneously, you position yourself not just for success in your current role but for expanding influence as an HR leader who addresses increasingly complex organizational challenges through the power of effective collaboration.

Will you treat collaborative problem-solving as a fundamental leadership approach or merely an occasional supplement to expert solutions? Your answer to this question may well determine whether your HR leadership creates temporary compliance or lasting organizational change.

CHAPTER 9:
BUILDING MOMENTUM THROUGH ACCOUNTABILITY AND TENACITY

THE MOMENTUM IMPERATIVE

"Vision without execution is hallucination. In HR leadership, your legacy won't be written in strategies you conceived but in transformations you completed."

The most brilliantly crafted HR strategy, developed with technical excellence, emotional intelligence, strong relationships, clear expectations, and collaborative engagement, will ultimately fail without one critical element— the tenacious execution and accountability that transforms vision into reality. While your knowledge, capabilities, and processes form the foundation of your HR leadership, your ability to build and sustain momentum determines whether your impact will be temporary or lasting.

For HR leaders specifically, momentum creation exists at a challenging intersection of direct and indirect influence. The function's broad organizational scope creates ambitious change aspirations, yet limited formal authority necessitates influence-based execution rather than directive implementation. The credibility gap that emerges when HR leaders articulate compelling visions without demonstrating tangible progress undermines both personal and functional effectiveness.

Despite its critical importance, momentum building remains one of the most overlooked leadership disciplines in HR. Some leaders focus exclusively on strategy development, assuming execution will naturally follow well-designed plans. Others launch multiple initiatives simultaneously without the focused accountability required for any to reach completion. Many fail to recognize how early wins create the credibility and energy essential for tackling larger transformations.

This chapter explores momentum building as the critical bridge between HR vision and organizational impact. We'll examine what distinguishes leaders who consistently translate strategies into outcomes from those whose initiatives fade into organizational memory without lasting change. You'll learn specific strategies for establishing accountability systems, creating momentum through strategic sequencing, overcoming inevitable implementation barriers, and building the personal tenacity required for sustainable HR leadership impact.

The uncomfortable reality is that even the most comprehensive leadership toolkit—technical expertise, emotional intelligence, relationship savvy, expectations mastery, learning agility, and collaborative skill—creates little value without execution momentum. The finest architectural plans are worthless without the disciplined construction that brings them to life. As the function responsible for developing accountability systems for others, HR must model the momentum-building discipline it promotes across the organization. The question isn't whether execution matters. It's whether you'll bring the same strategic focus to building momentum that you apply to developing vision.

THE MOMENTUM WAKE-UP CALL

Picture this...I had joined the district's risk management department during a period of significant change in educational safety protocols and compliance requirements. The department had a history of enthusiastically initiating safety programs and compliance processes—emergency response protocols, staff training initiatives, facility inspection programs—but it struggled with bringing them to full implementation across all schools in the district. Despite this pattern, I was eager to demonstrate my leadership value by introducing several innovative risk management initiatives simultaneously: a comprehensive safety audit process, an enhanced staff training program for emergency response, and a more structured incident reporting and tracking system.

Our risk management team created detailed plans for each initiative, conducted introductory sessions with school administrators, and launched the new approaches with district leadership endorsement. Initially, there was considerable interest and apparent momentum. I felt confident we were transforming the district's approach to risk management and safety.

Six months later, our implementation assessment revealed a troubling reality. Despite strong launches, adoption had stalled across all initiatives. School administrators had completed initial safety audits, but they weren't implementing the recommended changes. Staff participation in emergency response training had dropped significantly after the first sessions. The incident reporting system was being used inconsistently at best. Our ambitious risk management transformation agenda was quietly fading into the background of more immediate educational priorities.

Confused and frustrated, I sought guidance from a long-tenured facilities director known for successfully implementing district-wide changes. After listening to my explanation of our initiatives and implementation challenges, he offered wisdom that transformed my approach. He said, "You've launched three major programs simultaneously without establishing the support systems, accountability structures, or milestone tracking that enable busy school staff to sustain them. Your team is enthusiastically kicking off new programs, then moving on to launch the next one, leaving principals and teachers to maintain these efforts alongside their already overwhelming responsibilities."

This perspective catalyzed a complete reset of my approach. Rather than continuing to promote all initiatives simultaneously, I led a rigorous prioritization process with our risk management team that identified one critical initiative— the emergency response training program—as our primary focus. We established clear implementation milestones for each school, created straightforward accountability systems for principals and safety coordinators, and developed ongoing support mechanisms throughout the implementation journey. Most importantly, we committed to demonstrating visible success in all schools before launching any additional major initiatives.

The results of this focused approach were transformative. With concentrated attention and resources, the emergency response training program gained genuine traction across the district. Completion of early milestones created credibility that encouraged continued engagement from busy school staff. The visibility of real progress generated energy for addressing implementation challenges rather than quiet abandonment. Within four months, we had achieved greater implementation depth with one initiative district-wide than we had previously accomplished with three simultaneous efforts over six months.

This experience taught me that momentum isn't created through comprehensive plans or enthusiastic launches. It's built through focused execution, visible progress, and sustained attention that demonstrates commitment to completed implementation rather than just a focus on initiated programs. Most importantly, I learned that momentum isn't merely about working harder. It's about strategic sequencing, practical accountability systems, and implementation discipline that converts limited organizational energy and attention into maximum safety impact for students and staff.

THE THREE DIMENSIONS OF MOMENTUM MASTERY

Through both research and experience, I've identified three critical dimensions of momentum building that determine HR leadership effectiveness:

1. **Strategic Momentum Design**: Creating implementation approaches that generate progressive energy rather than resistance

2. **Accountability Architecture**: Establishing systems that drive consistent execution and visible progress

3. **Implementation Tenacity**: Developing the personal and team resilience required for sustained change effort

Let's explore each dimension with specific strategies for development.

STRATEGIC MOMENTUM DESIGN: ENGINEERING PROGRESS THAT ENERGIZES

Strategic momentum design focuses on deliberately structuring implementation approaches that generate energy through visible progress rather than depleting organizational resources through resistance and duplication. This dimension recognizes that how change is sequenced and paced dramatically impacts successful completion.

The HR Momentum Design Challenge

HR leaders face unique momentum design challenges due to their function's broad scope and indirect authority. The interdependent nature of HR initiatives creates complexity that can impede visible progress, while limited formal authority necessitates influence-based momentum rather than directive compliance. Additionally, HR changes often require behavior modifications from leaders at all levels, creating implementation dependencies beyond HR's direct control.

Strategies for Strategic Momentum Design

Establish rigorous approaches to focusing organizational energy.

Design implementation sequences that build progressive momentum.

Structure initiatives to create visible momentum through incremental achievements.

Develop approaches that minimize change resistance and maximize return on change effort.

Identify and address predictable resistance points before they emerge.

ACCOUNTABILITY ARCHITECTURE: BUILDING SYSTEMS THAT DRIVE COMPLETION

Accountability architecture focuses on establishing the systems, processes, and expectations that convert strategic intent into consistent execution. This dimension addresses the common challenge where early enthusiasm gradually dissipates without the structures required to sustain focused implementation efforts.

The HR Accountability Challenge

HR leaders face particular accountability challenges given their function's position as the organizational "accountability steward." The function responsible for performance management and accountability systems across the organization faces heightened expectations for demonstrating these disciplines within its own initiatives. Additionally, HR's matrix implementation approach—

where execution often depends on leaders outside direct authority—creates complex accountability requirements beyond what most functions encounter.

Strategies for Effective Accountability Architecture

Establish crystal clear ownership for implementation.

Develop robust approaches for tracking implementation progress.:

Implement structured approaches for accountability conversations.

Create systems that enable successful execution rather than just tracking it.

IMPLEMENTATION TENACITY: THE PERSONAL FOUNDATION OF MOMENTUM

Implementation tenacity focuses on developing the personal and team resilience required to sustain momentum through inevitable implementation challenges. This dimension addresses the reality that even perfectly designed initiatives encounter resistance, setbacks, and competing priorities that test leadership commitment.

The HR Tenacity Challenge

HR leaders face unique tenacity challenges due to their function's position and scope. The function's enterprise-wide impact creates implementation complexity that generates frequent setbacks, while its support orientation can create hesitancy to demonstrate the assertiveness sometimes required for implementation breakthrough. Additionally, HR's responsibility for multiple simultaneous initiatives creates attention fragmentation that can undermine sustained focus.

To address the unique challenges HR leaders face, it's crucial to adopt a strategic approach that balances assertiveness with the function's support-oriented role, while also managing multiple initiatives effectively. HR leaders can navigate this by prioritizing initiatives, aligning resources, and fostering cross-functional collaboration.

Three-Step Strategy:

1. Prioritize and Focus

Clearly define which initiatives align with the organization's highest strategic priorities. Establish a clear timeline and ensure that resources are dedicated to these initiatives, reducing fragmentation and maintaining sustained focus. Prioritization allows HR leaders to allocate resources efficiently and avoid the common pitfall of spreading attention too thinly across numerous projects.

2. Leverage Cross-Functional Collaboration

collaboration with key stakeholders across departments to ensure HR initiatives are supported throughout the organization. By involving operational leaders in the planning and execution stages, HR leaders can gain the assertiveness needed for successful implementation. This collaboration also ensures that HR solutions address the real-time needs of the organization, fostering buy-in and reducing setbacks.

4. Develop Structured Feedback Loops and Agility

Create regular feedback loops to assess the progress of ongoing initiatives and identify any potential obstacles early. This allows HR leaders to adjust strategies and demonstrate the assertiveness needed to overcome implementation challenges. Agility in execution—based on feedback—ensures that HR is responsive to organizational needs, helping to drive impactful change without being bogged down by setbacks.

By focusing on these three steps, HR leaders can better manage the complexity of their role, maintain a strategic focus, and assertively drive organizational change.

THE MOMENTUM MULTIPLIER EFFECT

An organization was pivoting from a traditional product manufacturing focus to a solutions-oriented approach that required different capabilities, mindsets, and organizational structures. As HR leader, I was responsible for developing and implementing talent strategies that would enable this transformation, including significant changes to selection, development, performance management, and organizational design.

The scope and complexity of this challenge dwarfed anything I had previously tackled. Initial planning revealed at least a dozen major HR initiatives required to support the transformation, each with significant implementation complexity. Using traditional approaches, full implementation would require years of sustained effort with a high risk of initiative fatigue and fragmented impact.

Drawing on hard-earned momentum lessons, I implemented an integrated approach that combined strategic momentum design, accountability architecture, and implementation tenacity in ways that created powerful multiplier effects. Rather than launching all required initiatives simultaneously, we created four sequential "transformation waves," each containing 2-3 highly connected initiatives with clear accountability and visible milestones.

For each wave, we established what we called a "momentum engine"—a cross-functional team with dedicated implementation capacity, clear responsibility mapping, and structured accountability reviews. These engines maintained an unrelenting focus on wave completion before moving to subsequent priorities. We implemented robust measurement systems that provided real-time implementation visibility, creating both accountability pressure and progress energy.

Most importantly, we developed team tenacity through deliberate resilience practices, including weekly reflection sessions, challenge navigation protocols, and compelling progress narratives that sustained energy through implementation difficulties. When obstacles emerged—as they inevitably did—these practices enabled persistence rather than surrender.

The results demonstrated the power of integrated momentum mastery. Implementation that would have required 3+ years using traditional approaches was substantially completed in 18 months. Each successful wave built credibility and organizational commitment that accelerated subsequent implementations. The visibility of tangible progress created energy that attracted additional resources and executive support, and the clear accountability architecture ensured that initiatives reached full implementation rather than remaining partially completed.

This experience taught me that momentum mastery isn't about isolated techniques but integrated systems that create virtuous cycles of progress, energy, and completion. Strategic design creates early wins that build credibility for accountability systems, which enable the sustained effort that drives implementation breakthroughs, which in turn builds the organizational confidence that enables more ambitious transformation. This momentum multiplier effect represents the highest expression of HR leadership execution capability.

THE MOMENTUM MASTERY FRAMEWORK: 90-DAY IMPLEMENTATION

I've developed an integrated framework for building momentum mastery during your first 90 days as an HR leader:

First 30 Days: Momentum Foundation

- Assess current momentum patterns for in-progress initiatives.
- Establish priority clarity for HR focus areas.
- Implement basic accountability systems for key initiatives.

- Model personal implementation discipline in your leadership approach.

- Create initial progress visibility through early milestone achievement.

Days 31-60: Momentum Acceleration

- Implement strategic sequencing for priority initiatives.

- Develop robust measurement systems for implementation tracking.

- Establish regular review disciplines for accountability conversations.

- Build team capacity for implementation tenacity.

- Create visible wins that demonstrate momentum capability.

Days 61-90: Momentum Sustainability

- Implement comprehensive momentum design for major transformations.

- Establish integrated accountability architecture across HR initiatives.

- Develop advanced barrier elimination systems for complex challenges.

- Build organizational recognition for implementation excellence.

- Create sustainable momentum rhythms that prevent initiative fatigue.

This framework ensures progressive development of momentum capability throughout your initial leadership period, moving from basic focus and accountability to sophisticated implementation systems.

Action Step: Create your "90-Day Momentum Mastery Plan" using this framework. For each phase, identify specific actions for developing your momentum capability and implementing momentum systems within your HR function. Review this plan weekly to assess progress and refine priorities.

MOMENTUM MASTERY: YOUR IMPLEMENTATION ADVANTAGE

As we conclude this chapter, it's essential to recognize that momentum mastery functions as perhaps your most fundamental leadership advantage as an HR leader. When you consistently translate vision into reality through focused execution and tenacious implementation, you establish both personal credibility and functional impact that distinguish you from leaders whose initiatives remain partially implemented or completely unrealized.

The HR leaders who create the greatest organizational impact aren't just technically proficient, emotionally intelligent, relationally skilled, expectation-savvy, learning-agile, and collaboratively excellent. They're momentum masters who reliably convert strategic intent into operational reality. They recognize that execution isn't peripheral to leadership effectiveness. It's the fundamental bridge between conceptual value and actual impact.

Your investment in momentum mastery isn't separate from your development as an HR leader. It's the critical capability that determines whether your other leadership dimensions create tangible organizational value. The strategies we've explored in this chapter directly impact your ability to implement the technical, emotional, relational, and collaborative aspects of HR leadership covered throughout this book. Without momentum mastery, even the most sophisticated HR approaches remain theoretical rather than transformational.

As you continue your HR leadership journey, commit to developing momentum mastery with the same dedication you bring to building other leadership capabilities. Regularly assess your implementation approaches, refine your accountability systems, and enhance your personal and team tenacity. Most importantly, build momentum into your leadership identity, approaching each initiative with execution excellence as a non-negotiable expectation rather than a hopeful aspiration.

The intersection of technical expertise, emotional intelligence, relationship mastery, expectation clarity, learning velocity, collaborative excellence, and momentum building creates a leadership foundation that translates potential into performance. By developing all dimensions simultaneously, you position yourself not just for respect as an HR strategist but for lasting impact as an HR transformer who consistently converts vision into value.

Will you allow the gap between concept and completion to limit your leadership legacy, or will you build the momentum mastery that bridges aspiration and achievement? Your answer to this question may well determine whether your HR leadership journey creates lasting transformation or merely temporary excitement.

CHAPTER 10:
THE PATH FORWARD:
BUILDING SUSTAINABLE HR
LEADERSHIP

THE INTEGRATION IMPERATIVE

"Sustainable HR leadership isn't about mastering individual capabilities. It's about integrating them into a coherent whole that transforms both your function and your organization."

Throughout this book, we've explored the critical capabilities that determine HR leadership effectiveness: elevated mindset, strategic onboarding, accelerated learning, day-one authority, emotional intelligence, team and relationship management, expectation mastery, collaborative problem-solving, and momentum building. Each capability forms an essential piece of the HR leadership puzzle, but the true power emerges not from excellence in any single dimension but from their integration into a leadership approach greater than the sum of its parts.

As you conclude your first 90 days and look toward sustained HR leadership impact, this final chapter focuses on integrating these capabilities into a coherent and sustainable leadership model. We'll explore how these dimensions reinforce each other, how you should continue developing your leadership toolkit beyond the initial transition period, and how you should create the organizational conditions that enable lasting HR transformation.

The most common mistake HR leaders make after successfully navigating their first 90 days is compartmentalizing leadership capabilities rather than integrating them. They apply an elevated mindset to some challenges while reverting to limited thinking on others. They demonstrate emotional intelligence in certain relationships while neglecting it in others. They build momentum on visible projects while allowing other initiatives to fade into the background. This inconsistent application creates a leadership ceiling that prevents the sustained excellence that characterizes truly transformative HR.

This chapter provides a framework for moving beyond transitional success to sustainable HR leadership impact. You'll learn strategies for creating virtuous leadership cycles where capabilities reinforce rather than compete with each other, approaches for continuous leadership development beyond your initial transition, and methods for embedding your leadership approach into HR function operations that outlast your individual tenure. Most importantly, you'll discover how to translate your first 90 days' foundation into a leadership legacy that creates lasting organizational value.

The journey from successful transition to sustainable impact requires moving beyond leadership capabilities as separate tools to an integrated leadership identity that transforms both how you lead and how your HR function creates organizational value. The question isn't whether you've developed the right capabilities during your transition. It's whether you'll integrate them into a coherent whole that enables truly transformative HR leadership.

THE LEADERSHIP INTEGRATION AWAKENING

My perspective on leadership integration crystallized during a pivotal moment in my HR leadership journey that revealed the transformative power of bringing together previously compartmentalized capabilities. This experience fundamentally shifted my understanding of sustainable HR leadership.

Several years into an HR leadership role in which I had successfully implemented numerous initiatives, I faced a profoundly challenging organizational situation. A combination of market pressures, leadership changes, and strategic shifts had created the perfect storm of people challenges: rising turnover, decreasing engagement, leadership capability gaps, and compensation competitiveness issues—all while the organization needed unprecedented workforce performance to address competitive threats.

Initially, I approached this situation as I had previous challenges by applying specific leadership capabilities to distinct problems. I leveraged my problem-solving expertise for the compensation issues, my relationship skills for the engagement challenges, my momentum building for turnover initiatives, and so on. While this approach created incremental progress on individual dimensions, the overall situation continued deteriorating despite my concentrated effort.

The breakthrough came during a moment of frustrated reflection when I realized I was creating unnecessary complexity by treating each challenge and capability as separate rather than integrated. I was applying relationships to engagement, momentum to turnover, and problem-solving to compensation as if they were distinct domains rather than interconnected elements of a unified system.

This realization prompted a fundamental shift in my approach. Rather than dividing challenges and capabilities into separate workstreams, I developed an integrated people strategy that addressed the entire talent ecosystem while leveraging all leadership capabilities simultaneously. Compensation changes were designed through collaborative problem-solving to enhance both retention and engagement. Leadership development incorporated accountability architecture that built implementation momentum. Engagement initiatives leveraged relationship networks to accelerate learning and application.

The results were transformative. Within six months, key people metrics showed significant improvement across all dimensions. Most importantly, the organization perceived HR as delivering an integrated solution rather than disconnected initiatives. The leadership team regularly commented on how our approach felt cohesive rather than fragmented, addressing systemic issues rather than symptoms.

This experience taught me that sustainable HR leadership impact doesn't come from excellence in individual capabilities. It comes from their integration into a cohesive approach. When leadership dimensions reinforce rather than compete with each other, they create a virtuous cycle that generates exponentially greater impact than the sum of individual capabilities. Most importantly, I learned that integration isn't merely an execution approach. It's a fundamental leadership mindset that transforms how HR creates organizational value.

THE FIVE DIMENSIONS OF INTEGRATED HR LEADERSHIP

Through research and experience, I've identified five critical dimensions of leadership integration that determine sustainable HR impact:

1. **Capability Alignment**: Ensuring different leadership capabilities reinforce rather than undermine each other

2. **Strategic Cohesion**: Creating unified HR approaches that address interconnected organizational challenges

3. **Functional Integration**: Building HR operating models in which specialized areas enhance rather than compete with each other

4. **Development Continuity**: Establishing ongoing leadership growth beyond the initial transition period

5. **Legacy Sustainability**: Creating enduring HR impact that outlasts individual leadership tenure

Let's explore each dimension with specific strategies for development.

CAPABILITY ALIGNMENT: CREATING VIRTUOUS LEADERSHIP CYCLES

Capability alignment focuses on ensuring that different leadership dimensions reinforce rather than conflict with each other. This dimension addresses the common challenge where growth in one capability inadvertently undermines effectiveness in another.

The HR Capability Alignment Challenge

HR leaders often experience tension between different leadership capabilities: the drive for collaboration conflicts with momentum requirements, expectations clarity creates relationship challenges, or problem-solving excellence competes with team development needs. These tensions can create leadership inconsistency that undermines overall effectiveness.

Strategies for Effective Capability Alignment

- Develop a comprehensive understanding of how your leadership capabilities interact.

- Establish approaches that deliberately combine capabilities for enhanced impact.

- Develop sophisticated approaches to navigating inherent capability tensions.

- Continuously adjust capability emphasis based on situational needs.

STRATEGIC COHESION: UNIFIED SOLUTIONS FOR COMPLEX CHALLENGES

Strategic cohesion focuses on creating integrated HR approaches that address interconnected organizational challenges. This dimension moves beyond addressing individual talent issues to developing unified strategies that recognize system interdependence.

The HR Strategic Cohesion Challenge

HR leaders frequently encounter problems that span traditional functional boundaries: performance issues connected to engagement challenges, recruitment difficulties tied to compensation constraints, or leadership gaps linked to cultural limitations. Addressing these challenges in isolation creates fragmented solutions that fail to resolve underlying systemic issues.

Strategies for Building Strategic Cohesion

Develop approaches for understanding organizational challenges as interconnected systems.

Create HR strategies that address multiple interconnected challenges simultaneously.

Implement coordinated approaches that maintain strategic connection during execution.

Assess impact through comprehensive frameworks that capture system-level outcomes.

FUNCTIONAL INTEGRATION: HR AS A UNIFIED SYSTEM

Functional integration focuses on building HR operating models in which specialized areas enhance rather than compete with each other. This dimension transforms HR from a collection of separate services to an integrated function that delivers cohesive organizational value.

The HR Functional Integration Challenge

HR functions frequently operate as loosely connected specialists—compensation, talent acquisition, learning and development, employee relations—with limited integration across domains. This functional fragmentation creates disconnected employee experiences, inefficient resource utilization, and diminished strategic impact.

Strategies for Enhancing Functional Integration

1. Integrated Operating Model Design

Create HR structures that facilitate functional connection.

Implement HR processes that connect across traditional boundaries.

Build team capabilities for cross-functional effectiveness.

Create a common purpose and identity that transcends functional specialization.

DEVELOPMENT CONTINUITY: BEYOND THE FIRST 90 DAYS

Development continuity focuses on establishing ongoing leadership growth beyond the initial transition period. This dimension transforms leadership development from a transition activity to a continuous practice that supports sustainable excellence.

The HR Development Continuity Challenge

HR leaders often experience a development plateau after their transition period. The focused growth that characterizes the first 90 days gives way to operational demands, creating stagnation in leadership capabilities that eventually limits effectiveness. Additionally, development often narrows to technical HR knowledge at the expense of leadership dimension growth.

Strategies for Maintaining Development Continuity

- Create structured approaches for ongoing leadership growth.

- Embed continuous development into regular leadership activities.

- Create systems that support long-term development vitality.

LEGACY SUSTAINABILITY :CREATING ENDURING IMPACT

Legacy sustainability focuses on creating enduring HR impact that outlasts individual leadership tenure. This dimension transforms HR leadership from personal effectiveness to institutional capability that creates sustainable organizational value.

The HR Legacy Sustainability Challenge

HR transformations frequently fail to sustain beyond the tenure of the leaders who initiated them. New approaches depend on the presence of specific individuals rather than becoming embedded in organizational systems, creating a cycle of initiative adoption and abandonment that undermines long-term effectiveness. Additionally, leadership transitions often trigger wholesale replacements of previous approaches rather than evolutionary improvement.

THE SUSTAINABLE HR LEADERSHIP FRAMEWORK

Based on research and experience, I've developed an integrated framework for building sustainable HR leadership capability beyond your initial transition:

First Year: Mastery Development

- Refine and deepen core leadership capabilities developed during transitions.

- Create integrated approaches that leverage capability combinations.

- Build HR team capability across critical leadership dimensions.

- Establish sustainable development practices for continuous growth.

- Create initial legacy systems that reduce leader dependency.

Years 2-3: Transformation Acceleration

- Implement integrated HR strategies that address systemic organizational challenges.

- Develop advanced capability combinations that create distinctive HR approaches.

- Build cross-functional excellence that transcends traditional HR boundaries.

- Create institutional capabilities that distribute critical competencies.

- Establish governance systems that maintain consistency through transitions.

Years 3-5: Legacy Establishment

- Embed key approaches into organizational culture and systems.

- Create comprehensive succession capability at multiple organizational levels.

- Build institutional knowledge management that preserves critical insights.

- Develop self-sustaining improvement systems that drive continuous evolution.

- Establish measurement approaches that maintain focus on sustained impact.

This framework provides a roadmap for translating initial transition success into sustainable HR leadership impact that creates enduring organizational value.

Action Step: Create your "Sustainable Leadership Plan" using this framework. Identify specific objectives and development activities for each timeframe, with particular focus on the first year beyond your transition. Establish quarterly review processes to assess progress and refine your approach.

THE INTEGRATED HR LEADER :YOUR GREATEST CONTRIBUTION

During my decades in HR leadership, I've observed that the greatest HR impact doesn't come from exceptional execution in any individual dimension but from the integration of capabilities into a coherent whole that transforms both the HR function and the broader organization. The most successful HR leaders I've known weren't necessarily the most brilliant strategists, the most emotionally intelligent coaches, or the most tenacious implementers. They were the most effective integrators who brought these capabilities together in ways that created sustainable organizational value.

My own journey of integration began with that pivotal moment when I realized I was creating unnecessary complexity by treating leadership capabilities and organizational challenges as separate domains, but it continued through years of deliberate practice integrating capabilities, building unified approaches, creating functional cohesion, maintaining development continuity, and establishing sustainable legacy. This journey transformed my leadership effectiveness far more profoundly than excellence in any individual capability ever could have.

The HR challenges facing organizations today—from talent competition to engagement dynamics to hybrid work environments to cultural transformation—demand integrated leadership approaches that address interconnected dimensions of organizational effectiveness. Technical knowledge remains important, and specific capabilities continue to matter, but sustainable impact requires the integration that transforms individual excellence into systemic transformation.

As you continue your HR leadership journey beyond your initial transition, I encourage you to embrace integration as your central leadership discipline. Rather than simply developing individual capabilities, focus on creating the connections between them that generate exponential impact. Rather than addressing discrete organizational challenges, develop unified approaches that leverage their interdependencies. Rather than building functional excellence in isolation, create the integrating mechanisms that transform HR into a cohesive strategic partner.

Your greatest contribution as an HR leader will not be found in any single initiative, capability, or approach. It will emerge from the integration that transforms both your function and your organization. By developing mastery in integration alongside your other leadership capabilities, you position yourself not just for short-term transition success but for the sustainable impact that defines truly transformative HR leadership.

Will you settle for excellence in individual capabilities or commit to the integration that creates truly transformative HR leadership? Your answer to this question will determine not just your immediate effectiveness but your enduring legacy as an HR leader who created sustainable organizational value.

EPILOGUE:
YOUR LEADERSHIP ASCENT BEGINS NOW

You are no longer the same professional who first opened this book. By now, you've shifted your mindset, reframed your perspective on leadership, and begun to see your HR career not just as a function—but as a mission. You've been given the blueprint to turn opportunity into impact, and uncertainty into clarity. Where others may still feel overwhelmed in transition, you now stand equipped with knowledge, strategy, and a renewed sense of purpose.

This transformation is more than theoretical. With this new understanding, you're positioned to fast-track your influence, establish credibility early, and drive meaningful change within your organization. The opportunity before you isn't just a stronger HR department—it's a more fulfilling career where you are seen, respected, and trusted as a true strategic leader. The tools you've gained will not only stabilize your first 90 days—they will elevate your leadership trajectory for years to come.

But transformation only happens when intention becomes action. It's not enough to read the playbook—you must implement it. The ideas you've encountered are more than leadership philosophies. They are practices designed to be lived. When you build a self-directed onboarding plan, elevate your mindset, and master your stakeholder relationships, the results will show in your team's performance, your executive influence, and your internal confidence. When applied, these strategies can reposition your role from HR manager to organizational change agent. It's that shift—from managing to leading—that defines the next level of your journey.

Let's revisit what you've learned—each chapter designed to build on the last, creating a complete system for HR leadership transformation:

- **Chapter 1: Understanding Why HR Leaders Fail**

  Reveals the four most common failure patterns in leadership transitions—and how to avoid them.

- **Chapter 2: The Elevated Mindset of Successful HR Leaders**

  Explores how your thinking determines your outcomes and introduces mindset shifts that unlock strategic leadership.

- **Chapter 3: Creating Your HR Leadership Onboarding Plan**

  Guides you in building a self-directed 30-60-90 day plan to accelerate learning, build credibility, and lead with purpose.

- **Chapter 4: Day One: Establishing Confidence and Authority**

  Provides a strategy for making a powerful first impression that positions you as a confident and credible leader from day one.

- **Chapter 5: Emotional Intelligence in HR Leadership**

  Shows how emotional intelligence becomes your greatest asset in navigating people dynamics and influencing at every level.

- **Chapter 6: Managing Team Dynamics and Key Relationships**

  Teaches how to cultivate team cohesion and build cross-functional relationships that amplify your leadership reach.

- **Chapter 7: Setting and Clarifying Expectations**

  Emphasizes the importance of clearly defined expectations to build alignment, accountability, and momentum.

- **Chapter 8: Problem-Solving and Fostering Collaboration**

  Equips you to lead through complexity using strategic thinking, structured collaboration, and conflict resolution.

- **Chapter 9: Building Momentum Through Accountability and Tenacity**

  Offers strategies to maintain forward movement, inspire follow-through, and create a results-driven culture.

- **Chapter 10: The Path Forward: Building Sustainable HR Leadership**

  Encourages long-term vision by defining what it means to lead with consistency, purpose, and a legacy mindset.

You've now got a comprehensive guide for your leadership ascent. But a guide is only as powerful as your willingness to use it. Implement what you've learned. Revisit these chapters often. Let your plan become your compass.

Let your mindset become your engine.

The runway is behind you. The sky is ahead.

You are not just an HR leader—you are a catalyst for culture, a builder of trust, and a steward of human potential. Your time is now. Your flight plan is clear. The next chapter of your leadership begins with a single step.

So take it—with courage, clarity, and confidence.

Welcome to your next level. The climb begins now.

ABOUT THE AUTHOR

Dr. Sheila Gilbert is a human resources expert, leadership strategist, speaker, and certified SHRM instructor who empowers emerging and established leaders to grow in confidence, competence, and credibility. With over 30 years of experience in public administration, education, and HR leadership, she is known for her ability to help professionals navigate complex workplace dynamics and lead with clarity and purpose.

Sheila is a proud graduate of Mississippi Valley State University, where she earned a Bachelor of Arts in Political Science. She also holds a Master of Public Administration, an Educational Specialist degree in Curriculum and Instruction, and a Doctorate in Business Administration. In recognition of her service in leadership and ministry, she was awarded an Honorary Doctorate in Biblical Studies. Additionally, she is SHRM-CP certified and a designated SHRM instructor who has helped hundreds of professionals earn their SHRM-CP and SHRM-SCP credentials.

Before launching her consulting firm, Sheila worked in higher education and local government, holding roles in leadership development, complaint resolution, and employee relations. Her professional journey includes leading organizational change, developing HR systems, and coaching high-potential leaders in both public and private sectors.

After years of helping organizations from the inside, Sheila founded **SG Consulting, LLC**, a boutique firm focused on HR strategy, leadership training, and professional development. She is the author of *The New HR Leader's 90-Day Playbook: Strategies to Grow Your Leadership and Impact Organizational Success*, a practical guide written to help new HR professionals build influence and navigate their first critical months in leadership.

From training bootcamps and executive retreats to certification prep and keynotes, Dr. Gilbert has become a trusted voice in the HR and leadership space. Her mission is to equip the next generation of HR leaders to not only succeed—but to shape the future of work.

She has coached over 600 HR professionals, inspired thousands through workshops and speaking engagements, and continues to develop tools, courses, and frameworks that empower others to lead with impact.

Her goal is to help leaders at all levels build strong teams, shape high-performing cultures, and leave a legacy of transformational leadership.

LEADERSHIP SOLUTIONS

Take your leadership to the next level. Our customized strategy solutions empower you to lead with clarity, inspire confidence, and achieve sustainable growth.

- Leadership Transformation Coaching
- Virtual Group Coaching
- Leadership Development
- Self-Directed Courses

Dr. Sheila Gilbert

Author | Coach | Consultant | Speaker

SHEILA GILBERT
LEADERSHIP STRATEGIST

WWW.DRSHEILAGILBERT.COM

www.ingramcontent.com/pod-product-compliance
Lightning Source LLC
Chambersburg PA
CBHW070931130626
46555CB00001B/385